INTERNATIONAL NEWS REPORTING

Pragmatics & Beyond

An Interdisciplinary Series of Language Studies

Editors:
Herman Parret
(Belgian National Science Foundation,
Universities of Louvain and Antwerp)
Jef Verschueren
(Belgian National Science Foundation,
University of Antwerp)

Editorial Address:
Department of Germanic Languages and Literatures
University of Antwerp (UIA)
Universiteitsplein 1
B-2610 Wilrijk
Belgium

Editorial Board:
Norbert Dittmar (*Free University of Berlin*)
David Holdcroft (*University of Leeds*)
Jacob Mey (*Odense University*)
Jerrold M. Sadock (*University of Chicago*)
Emanuel A. Schegloff (*University of California at Los Angeles*)
Daniel Vanderveken (*University of Quebec at Trois-Rivières*)
Teun A. van Dijk (*University of Amsterdam*)

VI:5

Jef Verschueren

International News Reporting:
Metapragmatic Metaphors and the U-2

INTERNATIONAL NEWS REPORTING:

Metapragmatic Metaphors and the U-2

Jef Verschueren
Belgian National Fund for Scientific Research
and
University of Antwerp

JOHN BENJAMINS PUBLISHING COMPANY
AMSTERDAM/PHILADELPHIA

1985

Library of Congress Cataloging in Publication Data

Verschueren, Jef.
  International news reporting.

  (Pragmatics & beyond, ISSN 0166-6258; VI:5)
Bibliography: p.
1. New York times. 2. American newspapers -- Language. 3. Foreign news -- United States. 4. U-2 Incident, 1960. 5. Metaphor. I. Title. II. Series.
PN4899.N42T587   1985   071'.471   86-11768
ISBN 90 272 2547 8 (European) / ISBN 0-915027-91-7 (US) (alk. paper)

© Copyright 1985 - John Benjamins B.V.
No part of this book may be reproduced in any form, by print, photoprint, microfilm, or any other means, without written permission from the publisher.

TABLE OF CONTENTS

PREFACE

1. THE FREE PRESS AS INEVITABLE TARGET ... 1
   - 1.0. Introduction ... 1
   - 1.1. The event ... 1
   - 1.2. The reporting ... 3
   - 1.3. The uptake ... 6
   - 1.4. Two predictions and a moral ... 7

2. LINGUISTS AND THE MEDIA: ELEMENTS OF A CIRCUS TRIAL ... 9
   - 2.0. Introduction ... 9
   - 2.1. Jalbert, Shaba, *Time*, and *Newsweek* ... 11
   - 2.2. Like-minded judges ... 25
   - 2.3. Relevant questions ... 30

3. A CASE STUDY: THE TOPIC ... 33
   - 3.0. Introduction: The U-2 incident ... 33
   - 3.1. Metapragmatic terms ... 34
   - 3.2. Metapragmatic metaphors ... 38
   - 3.3. The topic ... 39

4. A CASE STUDY: DATA AND COMMENTS ... 41
   - 4.0. Introduction ... 41
   - 4.1. May 6th ... 45
   - 4.2. May 7th ... 56
   - 4.3. May 8th ... 65
   - 4.4. May 9th ... 78
   - 4.5. May 10th to May 12th ... 81
   - 4.6. May 13th to May 16th ... 82

4.7.	May 17th	83
4.8.	May 18th to May 20th	91

5. A FUNCTIONAL ANALYSIS   93

5.0.	Introduction	93
5.1.	News reporting and truth	94
5.2.	News reporting and interpretation	96
5.3.	News reporting and understanding	97
5.4.	Misunderstanding: Whose responsibility?	99

FOOTNOTES   101

REFERENCES   103

INDEX   107

PREFACE

International news reporting is a highly complex communication process, often involving the use of language at two distinct levels: language is inevitably used in the actual reporting; and the reported events themselves may be basically communicative or dependent on verbal interaction. Thus news reports constitute a natural object for linguistic inquiry. Unfortunately, the more common types of linguistic approaches to the media show serious shortcomings. *First*, they tend to show a lack of familiarity with the structural and functional properties of the news gathering and reporting process in a free press tradition. The insights they gain are regrettably meager. As a case in point, the fact that international news reports usually reflect (at least an approximation of) the world views and value system dominant among the members of their target audience, is presented again and again as a major research finding whereas, in fact, it is simply predictable on the basis of those structural and functional properties. *Second*, the reasons for re-emphasizing the correspondence between reports and the predominant world view on every possible occasion, are mostly ideological rather than scientific. In the process of reaching the desired 'conclusion', linguistic articles on the media sometimes show stronger traces of ideological bias than the reports about which it is 'discovered' that they are ideologically biased. *Third*, as a cumulative effect of these two tendencies, the most interesting and challenging research questions are rarely asked. The double layering of the communication process, for instance, is generally ignored. And detailed accounts of what happens to linguistically encoded information on its communicative trajectory from event to report, are nearly impossible to find.

This brief monograph is intended as a contribution to the undoing of those flaws and to the maturation of linguists' partaking in the search for a better understanding of how the media in a democratic society can fulfill or fail to fulfill their task of providing information on international affairs. To this end, the first chapter offers some cursory background information on the free press and how it relates to a demand for objectivity. The second chapter discusses and criticizes some ideologically inspired approaches to the media as 'organizers of ideological production', and adds some hints on useful and relevant research issues. The remaining chapters contain an analysis of metapragmatic descriptions in reporting in *The New York Times* on the U-2 incident in May 1960; that is, a picture is presented of the way in which the Soviet and American verbal behavior constituting the core of this political-communicative event was described, and a functional analysis is given of the metapragmatic framing of the communicative exchange, with special attention to the use of metaphorical expressions.

This case study was undertaken in preparation of a wider, interdisciplinary, research project concerning U.S. reporting on the Soviet Union during the Khrushchev years, to be carried out in cooperation with Timothy McDaniel (Department of Sociology, University of California at San Diego). For the contents of this monograph, however, only the present author is to be held responsible.

1. THE FREE PRESS AS INEVITABLE TARGET

1.0. Introduction

Whoever thinks or writes about the news media must address the issue of objectivity or impartiality. Mostly, judgments about news reporting practices and standards are phrased in terms of this norm. Yet, as Michael Schudson puts it:

> "Objectivity is a peculiar demand to make of institutions which, as business corporations, are dedicated first of all to economic survival. It is a peculiar demand to make of institutions which often, by tradition or explicit credo, are political organs. It is a peculiar demand to make of editors and reporters who have none of the professional apparatus which, for doctors or lawyers or scientists, is supposed to guarantee objectivity." (M. Schudson 1978: 3)

There is, however, more to the peculiarity of this demand. *Webster's* defines the adjective *objective* as "belonging to nature or the sensible world; publicly or intersubjectively observable or verifiable esp. by scientific methods; independent of what is personal or private in our apprehension and feelings; of such nature that rational minds agree in holding it real or true or valid". Assuming that this is a reasonable reflection of what 'being objective' is generally intended to mean, the demand for objectivity in the reporting of any event involving people glosses over three levels of subjective human experience.

1.1. The event

First of all, the reported event can rarely be stated in terms of 'objective facts'. Even natural disasters become newsworthy mainly because they affect people's lives. Though some intersubjectively or verifiable facts can be given (such as the Richter scale measurement for an earthquake, the number of dead and wounded, the number of the homeless, an assessment of the damage in financial terms), other issues touch upon the complexities of human action and experience: the efficiency of rescue operations, the quality of aid for the victims (as viewed from the standpoint of those victims, or of the authorities), the responsibility for possible inadequacies in this respect. Industrial disasters (such as the escape of toxic gases from a chemical plant, or excessive radiation from a nuclear reactor), though some 'facts' can be verified, almost immediately lead to questions of responsibility and the wider issue of industrial policies, involving the viewpoints of the plant owners, managers and employees, the experience of the victims, their families and the community, and the interests of 'the economy'. Conflicts, as in industrial relations, have to be approached almost exclusively in terms of the often incompatible perpectives involved. And armed conflicts are less susceptible still to 'objectification'. Under conditions of war it may be impossible for a journalist to get access to the views, motives, and goals of one or more of the parties involved. And when access is available, it may be only through what is *said*.

Given the fundamental subjectivity of all social events, the notion of 'pure' objectivity, the idea that reporters should be able to present straightforward facts — and only those facts — died as soon as it was born. American journalists of the late nineteenth century, those responsible for the growth of *The New York Times*, were committed to facts, to the giving of information. But 'objectivity' did not belong to their vocabulary. The assumption was that facts could speak for themselves, without a context. The ideal of objectivity did not emerge until after World War I.[1] Its formulation was based on the realization that all previous reporting of 'facts' had indeed been embedded in a context, but a context that was simply taken for granted. Thus the explicit demand for objectivity (of the kind which even today constitutes the core of the concept as defined in *Webster's* and other dictionaries) immediately implied an awareness that it might be impossible to abstract from this first level of subjective human experience involved in news reporting, the level of the beliefs, emotions, and aspirations of those participating in the reported events.

To cope with this problem, some of the staunchest advocates of objectivity, such as Walter Lippmann, argued for the need to introduce scientifically accurate methods of news gathering and presentation. In theory it should be possible to offer a balanced picture of conflicting perspectives on controversial problems and events. The practical obstacles, however, are so immense that until today most attempts at 'objective reporting' on different points of view restrict themselves to a juxtaposition of direct quotations — if they can be obtained.

1.2. The reporting

The *second* level of human experience which the demand for objectivity tends to abstract from, involves the beliefs, opinions, hopes, and aspirations of those gathering, reporting, and publishing the news. Any market economy burdens the editors of a free press with concerns about economic survival, as is pointed out in the quote from Schudson (1978). Such concerns may motivate various degrees of sensationalism to accommodate a variety of established (or intended) audiences. Reporters are saddled with their editors' demands. Moreover, they are obliged to be gentle on their sources — if they don't want to lose them. Further constraints on both editors and reporters are imposed by a general code of professional ethics, which (certainly in the U.S.) involves loyalty to one's government (especially at times of crisis). A clear example of how such loyalty can be extended to allies was provided by the American press coverage of the Soviet Union during World War II. Criticism of communist Russia became much milder, and magazines such as *Collier's* and *Life* did their best to create a growing wartime pro-Soviet mood. Even in *The New York Times*, in editorial claimed on April 4, 1944, that "It is not misrepresenting the situation to say that Marxian thinking in Soviet Russia is out. The capitalist system, better described as the competitive system, is back."[2]

Loyalty to government policies can only be broken if it can no longer be justified on account of the 'national interest', or if hard evidence can be adduced which makes it unacceptable in a wider ethical context. Numerous illustrations are given by Tom Wicker in his book *On Press* (1975). For instance, the American press had been instrumental in the landslide victory of Lyndon B. Johnson over Barry Goldwater in the 1964 elections, by sinking its teeth into the latter's hawkishness and clinging to the former's repeated pledges that "he would not send American boys to fight an Asian war". Yet, a few months later, the same press was engaged in a tenacious struggle to explain that the same Lyndon B. Johnson had no choice but to dispatch American bombers to North Vietnam. Not until Harrison Salisbury of *The New York Times* visited Hanoi in 1966, did the American press feel free to judge the veracity of the administration's account of the bombings, purportedly aimed at military targets only. Not until 1966 did the press feel that it commanded a sufficiently hard core of evidence to justify a certain degree of 'disloyalty' which would ultimately make a significant contribution to the undoing of the war in Vietnam.

In addition to the general code of professional ethics, ideology inevitably co-determines what gets reported, when it is reported, and how the reporting is done. This is most visible in European party papers which usually make various forms of bias predictable, bearing the hallmark of the party ideologies involved. But also in the U.S., where party papers are mostly obscure, traces of ideology are easy enough to find. Their presence is less surprising than their absence would be, since language and thought are so intricately related. In this context, ideology should not only be seen as a more or less coherent framework of ideas and opinions which may color one's perceptions and one's ways of describing events. Also patterns of expectation and hopes are involved. A case in point, demonstrating how such factors may affect (international) news reporting, was the coverage of events during the Russian Revolution (from March, 1917, to March, 1920) in *The New York Times*, as examined by Walter Lippmann and Charles Merz in their classical "A test of the news" (1920). Lippmann and Merz were not out to crucify the *Times*. Rather,

> "The only question asked is whether the reader of the news was given a picture of various phases of the revolution which survived the test of events, or whether he was misled into believing that the outcome of events would be radically different from the actual outcome." (1920: 2)

A careful comparison of what was reported and the expectations that were created with what the reporters should and could have known at the time of the events, leads to the following summary of their conclusions:

> "The news as a whole is dominated by the hopes of the men who composed the news organization. They began as passionate partisans in a great war in which their own country's future was at stake. Until the armistice they were interested in defeating Germany. They hoped until they could hope no longer that Russia would fight. When they saw she could not fight, they worked for intervention as part of the war against Germany. When the war with Germany was over, the intervention still existed. They found reasons then for continuing the intervention. The German Peril as the reason for intervention ceased with the armistice; the Red Peril almost immediately afterwards supplanted it. The Red Peril in turn gave place to rejoicing over the hopes of the White Generals. When these hopes died, the Red Peril reappeared. In the large, the news about Russia is a case of seeing not what was, but what men wished to see." (1920: 3)

Far from accusing the *Times* of intentional misinformation, they add:

> "The chief censor and the chief propagandist were hope and fear in the minds of reporters and editors. [...] For subjective reasons they accepted and

believed most of what they were told by the State Department, the so-called Russian Embassy in Washington, the Russian Information Bureau in Paris, and the agents and adherents of the old regime all over Europe." (1920: 3)

A striking example — one of the many — was the reporting on Kolchak's anti-Bolshevik offensive in 1919. Though Kolchak was still more than five hundred miles from Moscow, and though he apparently needed eleven days to advance forty miles towards Samara and another six days to enter the city, this was presented as a 'drive on Moscow', and headlines informed the reader that "Kolchak pursues broken red army" and "Red rule totters as Kolchak wins".

Though more expert knowledge would certainly help reporters and editors to avoid such pitfalls, we are basically confronted with a limitless potential for human error. No matter how factual one tries to make the reporting of events, detaching it completely from one's frame of interpretations is impossible. It follows that seemingly 'objective' reports may on occasion be more misleading than if clear markers of interpretation would be embedded. This realization led to the growth of straightforward 'interpretive reporting' in the American press after World War I. One symptom of this was the introduction of weekend news summaries. Another was the invention of the syndicated political columnist. The feeling that facts could not be trusted as such and that the news needed to be explained, even produced new publications such as *Time* magazine (founded by Henry Luce and Briton Hadden in 1923).[3] Yet the division between editorials or news analyses (devoted to interpretive reporting) and 'objective' reports, has remained the accepted pattern in newspapers until today.

The problems that may arise from this strict division are aptly illustrated by the opening anecdote of Tom Wicker's *On Press*. Wicker tells us about a speech delivered by General Dwight D. Eisenhower during the Republican National Convention held in San Francisco's Cow Palace in 1964. The speech was a plea for party unity and was reported in that capacity as front page news, even though "by the time the convention opened, any good reporter knew that there was no Republican party unity and would be none that year" and though nobody seriously believed "that Dwight Eisenhower, for all his eminence, any longer wielded real influence in a party newly conquered by Barry Goldwater" (T. Wicker 1975: 3). More newsworthy than the 'political convention cliché' of an ex-president preaching party unity, was an event of a quite different nature. Eisenhower told the delegates that they should not let themselves be divided by those outside their family, including 'sensation-seeking columnists and commentators'. This remark sparked a barrage of angry shouts and raised fists at the reporters present. "In the first moments after Eisenhower's words, I feared some of the delegates might actually leap over the railing separating them from the press section and attack the reporters gazing in astonishment at this sudden surge of hatred." (2) The real significance of this event, the emergence of 'the press' as a participant in the political game rather than as a mere observer, could not be commented upon in the subsequent reports: "For a reporter to have drawn his own conclusions would have been 'editorializing in the news columns', the cardinal sin of objective journalism." (4) Wicker adds:

> "So at the moment when the hostility that the free American press aroused among its own readers first became dramatically apparent to the press itself, that press had so wrapped itself in the paper chains of 'objective journalism' that it had little ability to report anything beyond the bare and undeniable fact that the Republican National Convention had 'fairly exploded' at Eisenhower's words." (4)

Little seems to have changed since 1964.

1.3. The uptake

Demands for objectivity also simplify a *third* level of human experience, involving the subjectivity of the news 'consumers'. As all editors (not only newspaper editors) know, texts have to be adapted to the (intended) audience in much the same way as speech gets adapted to one's hearer(s) (in terms of shared knowledge which can be relied upon, common assumptions of a prejudiced or unprejudiced nature, social relationships between speaker and hearer, etc.). 'Public opinion' has been too exclusively presented as a product of the news media. Not only policy makers, but also journalists have to be attuned to is. Reporters and editors cannot afford to shake public opinion without irrefutable evidence, which is usually hard to come by. Thus positing a one-directional causal link between attitudinal changes in the press and attitudinal changes in the general public, may grossly distort the picture. Did the average American become more favorably inclined towards the Russians as a result of more positive reporting during World War II? Or did the reporting become more positive not only because this was in the 'national interest', but also because the general public might not have tolerated the continuation of harsh criticism directed at a major ally in a war in which American blood was flowing? A negation of the disjunction is probably the key to a realistic answer to these questions.

The concept of objectivity hinges on the notion of intersubjective observability and verifiability. Considering the problem from the audience's point of view, our third level of human experiencee involved, the ideal is nothing short of an illusion. The vast majority of readers is almost never in a position to observe or verify any of the events reported. Yet they play an active role in the process of information transfer. Their reading is guided by selective attention based on their personal interests. And their own frame of interpretation — or set of biases, if one prefers a less flattering term — is responsible for the differential weight attached to aspects of a story which may have been given equal prominence by the journalist. Other things they may choose to forget or refuse to believe. No matter how closely a reporter manages to approach the ideal of objectivity, what remains after a report has been digested by its readers is virtually impossible to control. And apart from assigning a story to the front page with a catchy title, also an editor can do little to influence the process of reader uptake.

1.4. Two predictions and a moral

To add to the complexity, the three levels of human experience involved in the functioning of the news media (the level of those participating in the events, the level of those responsible for the reporting, and the level of news 'consumers') are constantly intertwined. As is clear from Tom Wicker's Cow Palace anecdote, the news media may become actors in the events to be reported, participants in the political game. This is why Belgian Christian Democrats and Liberals are constantly complaining that there are too many Socialists in key positions at the Belgian Radio and Television network. Conversely, government agencies and businesses have turned themselves into reporters by flooding the press with information. Public relations activities and press releases serve this type of 'news management'. Another form of news management blurring the boundaries between the levels of human experience, is the creation of 'pseudo-events', events orchestrated for the sole purpose of their being reported. Notorious examples are the interview and the press conference. But these are only the most transparent ones.

All the subjectivities structurally embedded in the workings of the free press, allow us to formulate two predictions. One concerns its content, the other its reception.

About the content of the free press we can predict that, in general, its major instruments (the most authoritative or most widely distributed papers and magazines) will reflect an average picture of the world view, ideology, and values prevalent in the society in which it functions. Far from being a sign of manipulatory deviousness, this is due to the same fundamental properties of natural language and social interaction which enable us to draw inferences about assumptions of mutual knowledge and shared values from the structure of verbal exchanges in everyday conversations. Yet, this phenomenon is worthy of close scrutiny because of the perseverance of a naïve and somewhat paradoxical assumption of objectivity. Dan Schiller says:

> "Invoked conventionality, objectivity ostensibly precludes the very presence of conventions and thus masks the patterned structure of news: it is an invisible frame." (1981: 2).

The frame is not really invisible. But seeing it requires special attention.

We can also predict that all the subjectivities involved will make the free press into an inevitable target for criticism. If it tries to do a reasonably good job, it will be under fire from various (often opposing) sides. While the critical culture of the 1960s attacked the press for its reflection of governmental viewpoints and assumed majority values, conservatives did not hide their disenchantment with its incipient assimilation to the 'adversary' ideology. And while government officials tend to chastise reporters for their role in 'leaking' state secrets, others would like to hang them for withholding information. In a sense, the amount and variety of criticism directed at the press is indicative of the quality of its reporting.

Since "the reliability of the news is the premise on which democracy proceeds" (W. Lippmann and C. Merz 1920: 4), careful, dispassionate, and continuous investigation of the media's performance is a must. The moral to be drawn from the foregoing considerations, however, is that nothing is easier than to criticize the press. The task it faces is extremely complex, so that it is hard to imagine higher standards of reporting than those achieved by some of the giants in the field of journalism, such as Walter Lippmann or Harrison Salisbury, to name just two. Research, therefore, may serve the purpose of upgrading the general quality of news reporting, but it should be primarily aimed at making better readers, readers able to see through (if not see) the 'invisible' frame which necessarily patterns the news.

2. LINGUISTS AND THE MEDIA: ELEMENTS OF A CIRCUS TRIAL

2.0. Introduction

Most newsworthy social events involve the use of language. Moreover, the process of information transfer called 'reporting' is basically a matter of institutionally constrained language production and comprehension. These are two reasons why the news media form a natural topic for linguistic research. The first one, involving a meta-level of analysis, is usually forgotten. The second one has led to a disappointingly meager harvest of research results, disproportionate to the bulk of writings it has engendered. Just consider the following quote from a chapter on news ideology in *More Bad News* by the Glasgow University Media Group (1980: 122):

> "News talk occurs within a cultural framework which stresses its balance and impartiality. Yet despite this, detailed analysis reveals that it consistently maintains and supports a cultural framework within which viewpoints favourable to the *status quo* are given *preferred* and *privileged* readings."

This observation is generally accurate. But rather than being a profound insight derived from detailed analysis, the conclusion is entirely predictable from the structural properties of the workings of the free press, as we have shown in the first chapter. The results of detailed analysis can be usefully invoked to confirm such a prediction. But presenting it, over and over again, as a major research finding, diverts the attention from a more interesting question: What communicative mechanisms enable the news media, in spite of their being 'anchored' in a common ideological ground, to 'inform' its audience, to provide new insights and, on occasion, to contribute to attitudinal changes? A realistic answer cannot be given without observing that the conjunction 'in spite of' betrays an unwarranted bias. Linguists should have learnt from the study of everyday conversation that communication is not even possible without a common ground. Why should a different dictum hold for the type of communication involved in news reporting?

It is hard to avoid getting the impression that almost all linguistic studies of the news media are intended to put the media on trial. After another 'detailed analysis', this one focusing on the (television) reporting (in Britain, Germany, and the USA) of the Aldo Moro kidnapping and murder case in 1978, Howard Davis and Paul Walton (1983: 48) conclude:

> "The visual and verbal content of the Moro news story tells more about the maintenance of an ideologically safe version of consensus by media demarcation than it does about the 'events' which constitute the news."

This observation shows clearly that presenting the world view (called 'consensus' here) underlying news reports as a major research discovery, precludes asking further questions. The media are found 'guilty'. The trial is closed.

Even for those unaware of the predictability involved, suspicions of an unfair trial should be aroused by the frequency of another type of conclusion. Consider the following passage from Gunther Kress (1983: 134-135).

> "The expression of the writer's attitude towards the proposition contained in a sentence has been discussed above. On the face of it this seems to have nothing to do with interpersonal meaning. That is, if speaker/writer and hearer/reader are related by a message, we expect some reference (however implicit) to aspects of the speaker-hearer relation. However, the situation is one where the paper speaks to its readers with the intention to inform them, ostensibly at least. Hence one aspect of interpersonal meaning is to achieve solidarity between the paper's point of view and the reader's. In such a framework it is clear that the writer's expressed attitude to the proposition does have interpersonal effect. It represents an attempt to structure the reader's interpretation of the event, and to bring him or her into agreement with the paper's ideology."

In other words, the same press which was convicted of simply reflecting the prevailing ideology without really giving information, is presented as a devious manipulator trying to impose its own ideology on those innocent members of society called 'readers'. Clearly, something is wrong. To the extent that the press is rooted in a common world view and the socially dominant values, this is presented as dishonesty hidden behind the professed aim of providing information. To the extent that there is a relationship of influence between the press and its readers, it is depicted unidirectionally, from press to reader, as an attempt at manipulation. The jurors (if not the judge) seem to have established the defendant's guilt in advance, determined to hang him, even if it would take contradictory charges to bring this about.

From scientific analyses one should expect a more balanced picture. But not only is the trial unfair. In most cases a downright circus trial is held. Let us take a detailed look at one case.

2.1. Jalbert, Shaba, *Time*, and *Newsweek*

In "Some constructs for analysing news", Paul L. Jalbert (1983) sets out to show how 'ideological work' is involved in news media presentations. The diagnosis is formulated in the first paragraph.

> "Ideology is seen to be a routine feature of the social production of news stories which is congruent with political and economic interests, organized and unorganized. The mass media are seen to occupy a significant place as organizers of ideological production." (Jalbert 1983: 282)

As his main sample for analysis, Jalbert takes the *Time* and *Newsweek* articles of May 29, 1978, on the invasion earlier that month of Zaïre's Shaba Province by Katangan rebels. The article is intended to identify "certain devices which enable us to see just what ideology-as-presented involves" (282). Jalbert continues:

> "These devices and procedures include (1) membership categories and their selection options, (2) the exploitation of the reifying character of synecdochic and metonymic constructions, (3) *de re/de dicto* transformations, (4) the juxtaposition of transparent descriptions for opaquely true descriptions, and (5) the analysably distinct orders of presupposition." (282)

The remainder of this section will be devoted to a sentence-by-sentence commentary of the first three pages of Jalbert's analysis, in which he adduces the bulk of his evidence to support the first count (dealing with membership categorization) of his five-point indictment. These pages are highly representative of the quality of Jalbert's approach. Thus treating the whole article this way would be redundant.

Obviously, it is impossible to talk about people, events, and circumstances without categorizing. Moreover, the categories one chooses are indicative of one's attitudes to the people referred to and one's interpretation of the events and circumstances. Jalbert makes this point with reference to Harvey Sacks's (1972: 32) definition of 'categorization devices'. He adds:

> "Although Sack's [sic!] observations were based on conversational interactions, they have clear relevance to media studies because it is fair to expect that organizations and their representatives also select categories in strategic, although unreflective ways." (283)

It is unclear why the question of 'fairness' is raised when stating the obvious. Is this meant to justify the jump from Sacks's observations about the inevitability of categorization in everyday life to the media's "strategic [should we read: '(somewhat) devious'?], although unreflective" selection of categories? But, so far so good.

After these general remarks, Jalbert embarks on the analysis of a first extract from *Newsweek's* account of the events in Zaïre's Shaba Province:

> "MASSACRE IN ZAIRE
> Zaïre's President Mobutu Sese Seko stared through the window of a mining-company guesthouse in the shattered city of Kolwezi. The battlehardened President, a former army sergeant, put his hands to his face and moaned: "*Mon Dieu*, they have smashed their heads in." Inside the guesthouse, 35 European men, women and children lay dead. They had been herded into a room and executed by Katangan invaders before the attackers themselves were driven out of town by the French Foreign Legion.
> The ghastly massacre in Kolwezi came hours before a gallant rescue effort. By last week, it appeared that more than 100 white hostages had been butchered by Katangan rebels — but that nearly 3,000 more had been saved by the French legionnaires and Belgian paratroopers who flew in, with American help, to prevent a slaughter that might have been even worse. [...] Armed with Soviet weapons and apparently trained by Cuban advisers, the Katangans drove Zaïre's troops out of Kolwezi and kept them out. [...]" (*Newsweek*, p. 34, cols. 1-2)

Jalbert's first comment runs as follows:

> "The text reads as if it were an eye-witness account of the events depicted, which may enhance the credibility of the report. It seems that the reporter is in the presence of President Mobutu (although this is not made explicit) because he reports that Mobutu puts 'his hands to his face' and quotes him directly." (283)

Most readers of news weeklies — apparently excluding Jalbert — know that staff writers 'producing' the published version of urgent news items can rarely be regarded as the 'authors' of the text. Their task consists in piecing together reports which they receive from international news agencies, staff correspondents, and reporters in the field. As a result, portions of a text which 'read as if they were an eye-witness account' usually *are* eye-witness accounts. In the case under investigation, the 'reporter' involved does not only *seem* to be in the presence of President Mobutu, but he *is*. Moreover, contrary to Jalbert's contention, this *is* made explicit. Not just once, but in four different ways! First, the article is signed "RAYMOND CARROLL, with JAMES PRINGLE in Kolwezi, JAMES O. GOLDSBOROUGH in Paris, and bureau reports" (*Newsweek*, p. 40, col. 3). Second, in the "Top of the Week" summaries (p.3) the last line on the events in Zaïre reads: "Two days before the rescue, Zaïre's President Mobutu flew a planeload of reporters — including Newsweek's James Pringle — into Kolwezi to demonstrate his determination to repel the invaders (page 36)." Third, in the introduction to the half-page explicit eye-witness insert "Flight to Kolwezi" (on p. 36), to which the quoted summary sentence refers, we find further information on James Pringle's presence at the scene of the events:

> "For NEWSWEEK's James Pringle, flying to beleaguered Shaba Province in a C-130 with President Mobutu Sese Seko at the controls is becoming old hat. He did it once in 1977 when Katangan rebels occupied part of the province — and twice during the fighting last week. The first flight to Kolwezi came the day before French and Belgian troops launched their rescue mission, and Mobutu's party spent a scant twenty minutes on the ground. Pringle's report: [...]." (*Newsweek*, p. 36, col. 1)

This suggests that Pringle's reports inserted in the main article are based on what he saw when he personally visited Kolwezi for the second time the same week, with President Mobutu, after the rebels had been driven out of town. Fourth, this suggestion is turned into an explicit statement within the main article itself:

> "Hours after the operation [by French and Belgian troops] began, Newsweek's James Pringle flew into Kolwezi with a party of journalists aboard a plane copiloted by Mobutu himself. Pringle's report: [...]." (*Newsweek*, p. 34, col. 3, to p. 35, col. 1.)

What follows is an integrated first-person direct report by Pringle (continuing up to p. 39) in which he says, for instance: "I stood alongside President Mobutu as he looked into the guesthouse where the 35 bodies were sprawled, [...]." (*Newsweek*, p. 36, col. 3). This information is only absent for those who really do not want to see it.

The analysis continues:

> "This impression [the impression that the text seems like an eye-witness account] carries through right into the report of the incidents: 'They had been herded into a room and executed ...'." (p. 283)

This comment shows Jalbert to be oblivious to the fact that the concord of tenses in English dictates the use of the past perfect for events prior to a past moment of observation. As if this were not enough, the quoted sentence continues with further details situating the event in time: "[...] before the attackers themselves were driven out of town by the French Foreign Legion." Under normal circumstances, only someone who does not understand English properly could be expected to accuse the writer of the *Newsweek* article of trying to create the impression that he (or the reporter whose story he relies on) was a direct witness to the events described. These events are unambiguously presented as the cause of a state of affairs which *is* directly observed by a *Newsweek* reporter.

So far nothing was said about membership categorization in the first extract. But after the preliminary sortie just presented, Jalbert turns to the focus of this section.

> "The word 'herded' is used without qualification, implying that the people were treated as subhuman, as cattle, and later the word 'butchered' maintains the metaphor, although we have no *direct* evidence of these events." (283-284)

Conceivably, the people were already together in the room before they were discovered by the rebels who killed them. Apart from this possibility (maybe excluded by the reporter on the basis of eye-witness accounts) which would render 'herd together' inaccurate, there is little reason to criticize the choice of metaphor. Indeed, describing the smashing in of people's heads or any other method of executing civilians— men, women, and children—as a non-subhuman treatment would require a more aberrant world view. It is a peculiar demand to ask for more direct evidence than even a glimpse of the resulting picture.

The next sentence reads:

> "The report makes a significant juxtaposition between Mobutu, who is described as a sympathetic observer ('he moaned') and as being identified with the Zaïrian masses ('a former army sergeant'), and the 'ghastly massacre' caused by these 'attackers'." (284)

Unless Jalbert wants to dispute the fact of the 'massacre', unless he really stands behind the implication that the event was not 'ghastly', unless he really means that it is wrong to classify rebels invading an established national territory as 'attackers', there is little reason to find fault with *Newsweek's* categories. The passage referred to is intended to describe Mobutu's reaction to the scene depicted. No matter what atrocities one may hold his regime responsible for (some of which are explicitly mentioned further on in the report; e.g. p. 40, col. 1), Mobutu may indeed have been a 'sympathetic observer' in the face of the 'ghastly massacre'. Had he acted indifferently, this would have been reported too. But where Jalbert's analysis completely derails is in attributing an 'identification with the Zaïrian masses' to the descriptive phrase 'a former army sergeant'. Where, or since when, are army sergeants identified with the masses of a population? The only function of the phrase is to explain the adjective 'battlehardened'. And jointly, the adjective and its justification serve to emphasize that even someone who has probably seen horrible scenes before in life, was shocked by what he observed through the window of that mining-company guesthouse in Kolwezi. Elsewhere in the report, whenever Mobutu's background is mentioned, the rendering is more complete, including an aspect which would have been more conducive to an identification with regular people: 'a former journalist and sergeant in Belgium's Congolese Army' (p. 36, col. 3; p. 40, col. 1). And that Mobutu is not to be regarded as your ordinary kind of guy, is made very explicit:

> "Since I saw him last [...] he [Mobutu] has even shown signs of incipient modesty: he no longer appears, descending from a cloud, at the start of television programs, and recently he has taken to wearing the insignia of a three-star general, instead of his customary four stars." (*Newsweek*, p. 36. col. 3)

The irony should be clear.

But unrelentingly, Jalbert continues his indictment, introducing a new count with every new sentence.

> "The Kantangan people are referred to as 'invaders' and 'rebels'. The category 'rebels' creates an affiliation between its members and the territory on which they are fighting. The category 'invaders' strongly implies that its members are not affiliated with but imposing force on the territory. Who are the Katangan people and where do they come from?" (284)

Who refers to the Katangan *people* as 'invaders' and 'rebels'? Surely not the author of the *Newsweek* article. He talks *only* about Katangan *invaders* and Katangan *rebels*, not about the people. Though there must, of course, be some sort of association with the Katangan people, Jalbert's vision of an automatic one-to-one correspondence must be the product of a rather peculiar view of the world. And what about the categories 'invaders' and 'rebels', about which it is suggested that they are incompatible, or even contradictory? The report explains quite clearly why both characterizations, and not just one of them, apply. Significantly, the whole explanation, details of which are spread out all over the text, is crystallized in one sentence left out (purposefully or not) from Jalbert's first extract from *Newsweek*. At the place of the first three dots, the text says:

> "Kolwezi's agony began the week before, when perhaps 2,000 Katangans — losers of the former Belgian Congo's civil war twelve years ago — slipped into Zaïre from their sanctuaries in Angola and swiftly captured Kolwezi and the town of Mutshatsha, 65 miles away." (*Newsweek*, p. 34, col. 1)

This teaches us that twelve years before (in 1966), the Katangans were involved in, and lost, a civil war. Since a 'civil war' is defined as a war between factions or regions of one country, they must be Zaïrians themselves. And since those Katangans who captured Kolwezi in May 1978 obviously still refuse allegiance to, and oppose by force, the established government or ruling authority, the catogory 'rebel' is quite appropriate. Moreover, those Katangans who still want to rebel have found a sanctuary in neighboring Angola. They launched their offensive from across the border. Hence they are also 'invaders'. In this context, the second conjunct of Jalbert's "Who are the Katangan people and where do they come from?" can only be treated as a mock question. The first conjunct, however, is a very serious one, though its relevance is undermined by Jalbert's identification of the people with the rebels, and though Jalbert certainly does less to provide an answer than the *Newsweek* text which is implicitly accused of not answering it. Some background information is offered, as in the following lines:

> "The invading force is one of the more curious armies on the African continent. In the 1960s, the Katangans fought for secession under the late Moise Tshombe, and at that time they were considered to be politically right-wing. After Tshombe's rebellion was put down, they found refuge in Angola, and during the 1970s the exiles — now numbering more than 200,000 by some estimates — forged an alliance with Marxist Agostinho Neto, now President of Angola." (*Newsweek*, p. 39, col. 1)

More historical details would certainly have been desirable. For instance to clarify the name 'Katangans', which derives from a previous name for Zaïre's Shaba Province, Katanga, which was declared independent by Moise Tshombé on July 11, 1960 (eleven days after the official independence day for the former Belgian Congo), and which kept opposing the authorities in Kinshasa until its capitulation in January 1963 (after a decisive offensive by UN troops). The report could have explained, in support of the claim about the right-wing character of secessionist Katanga, that Tshombé was supported by a white mercenary army and that Belgium provided him with covert military and technical assistance inspired by Belgian mining interests. It could have been explained that there is no 'natural unity' to Katanga, now Shaba; that it consists of three major ethnic groups, the Luba, Lunda, and Bemba; that not all Luba, Lunda, and Bemba territories are included in the province; that Tshombé belonged to a Lunda tribe and was not unanimously supported by all Katangans (as attested by, for instance, a revolt by the Baluba tribe against his secessionist regime in August 1960); that most of the Katangans operating from Angola were Lundas; that the only proper claim to unity for

Katanga is captured in its new name, Shaba, the Swahili word for 'copper' (though the abundance of minerals in the Shaba region does not only include copper, but also cobalt, zinc, coal, silver, cadmium, gold, palladium, platinum, etc.) and that this is an important reason for prime time international interest in the area. Of all these facts, only the latter, crucial as it may be to an understanding of the events, gets the attention it deserves in the *Newsweek* report.

Jalbert's next sentence drags out the issue of the identification of the Katangans.

> "Further, the reporter reifies the Katangan rebels by referring to them merely as 'Katangans'. By contrast, other forces are referred to in full as organised forces, for example, the 'French *Foreign Legion*', 'French *legionnaires*', the 'Belgian *paratroopers*' and 'Zaïre's *troops*'." (284)

'Reification' is the materializing of abstractions.[4] The alchemy required to reify Katangan rebels, supposedly already made up of flesh and blood, must invoke the blackest of black art. Moreover, the accusation that the French and the Belgians are referred to as organized troops whereas the Katangans are not (a practice for which easy justification could be found in the explicitly described unclear status of the rebel force), is based on incomplete homework. The French are also referred to as 'the French', and the Belgians as 'the Belgians'. Conversely, there is talk about 'Katangan *soldiers*' and 'Katangan *troops*', and the rebel force is identified as the 'Congolese National Liberation Front'. An attempt is made to avoid the term 'Zaïrians' which, if not handled carefully, might have blurred the Zaïrian origin of the Katangans themselves.

The topic switches now to the question of Soviet and American involvement.

> "The reference to 'Soviet weapons' suggests that there is a political and military tie with the Soviet Union; whereas we are told that there was some 'American help', which leaves us wondering what kind of help the Americans provided in the face of such a 'slaughter that might have been even worse'. The contrast is made between the specific character of the word 'weapons' (which carries with it aggressive connotations) and the openendedness of the word 'help' (which implies a kind of humanitarian commitment). However, the 'help' the Americans rendered could have itself consisted of weapons." (284)

Who is left wondering what kind of help the Americans provided? Not the average reader of the *Newsweek* text. Any benevolent reader would have thought of logistic support (which has military, though non-combatant, rather than 'humanitarian' connotations), even without further explicit clues. As it happens, however, there is even an abundance of such clues. In the "Top of the Week" summary (p. 3), it is said that "The rescue operation was supported by U.S. transport planes, as Jimmy Carter took a tougher stand against Soviet-Cuban adventurism in Africa [...]." And the sentence directly following the extract quoted by Jalbert, says:

> "In view of the threat to the European hostages — and to Kolwezi's copper mines — France and Belgium decided to send in troops, with American planes ferrying fuel and supplies to the edge of the combat zone." (*Newsweek*, p. 34, cols. 2-3.)

A further indication:

> "Although Carter placed the 82nd Airborne Division on alert, it was decided that no American combat units would be sent to the war zone. Instead, U.S. planes would fly fuel and supplies to Zaïre for use by the Belgians and French. "The U.S. isn't holding the baby", said NATO secretary-general Joseph Luns, "But one might say they are pushing the pram." The other allied nanny was Britain, which sent four RAF transport planes to Kamina, 125 miles north of Kolwezi, to help evacuate foreigners." (*Newsweek*, p. 39, col. 3.)

Theoretically, 'supplies' might indeed have included weapons, though one may safely assume that the Belgian and French paratroopers flown in were properly armed for the job, especially given the status of both the Belgians and the French as notorious arms dealers. No attempt is made to hide or downplay the more active involvement of the western powers as compared to the Soviet Union. The Soviets only provided the weapons. The Cubans trained the rebels on the territory of Marxist Angola, and intelligence reports are cited in support of the claim that Cuban advisers trucked them up to the Zaïrian border. The training is said to have been good enough for them to discipline each other for stealing from citizens, until discipline broke down when they started drinking. In contrast, some western powers sent in their own combat units. And though this is presented as a 'gallant rescue effort', no attempt is made to cover up the less unselfish motive of protecting vested interests in this economically important region. A reporter really trying to create or capitalize on strong anti-communist sentiments, could easily have insinuated that the copper mines, rather than Shaba's liberation from Mobutu's dictatorship, were central to Angola's, Cuba's, and Russia's interests in the cause of the Katangan rebels. There is, however, no trace of

this in the text.
Jalbert concludes his discussion of the *Newsweek* extract as follows:

"One final observation about this article is that the Katangese account is excluded from it. The upshot is that the Katangan people are indicted on the basis of a supposedly factual account of the situation. It is clear that in reading this story the reader might arrive at some mistaken conclusions. It is the manner in which the news is presented that plays the crucial role in the way that information will be understood by the reader. The selection of categories and the ordering of these selections is paramount; for, whether explicitly or implicitly, they carry with them content and meaning which create a message congruent with the beliefs of the author." (284)

Frankly, there is nothing interesting in this conclusion. First, by the time any reporter could be reasonably expected to reach Kolwezi (unless they had been invited to accompany the rebels when they launched their attack), the Katangans had left: their own account was not directly available. Second, no-one is indicting the Katangan *people*. Nor are the Katangan rebels indicted for their rebellion as such. On the contrary, to the extent that motives are dealt with, only those are presented which the Katangans would certainly not want to deny: the original aim was secession for Shaba Province, but the wider goal of putting an end to Mobutu's dictatorship in general is also apparent. The Katangan rebels *are* indicted for the brutalities they committed, on the basis of an undeniably factual account. Third, readers are unlikely to arrive at those mistaken conclusions which seem to dominate Jalbert's interpretation. Fourth, *of course* information can only be understood on the basis of the manner in which it is presented. Finally, discourse conventions (including categorization devices) aimed at creating a message *in*congruent with the beliefs of the author, would be highly undesirable. Yet I hope Jalbert is using such unorthodox conventions when he announces the topic of his *Newsweek* excerpt as "the tumult caused by the Katangan rebels who entered the Shaba Province of Zaïre in May 1978" (283). Or does Jalbert really believe that *his* categories (more appropriate to "the tumult caused by the circus wagons that entered the city for the annual fair") give a more objective picture of the events?

Jalbert goes on to analyze an excerpt from the *Time* magazine issued the same week. The excerpt:

"THE SHABA TIGERS RETURN
[...] An estimated 5,000 Katangese guerrillas of the Congolese National Liberation Front (F.I.N.C.) [sic][5], which has been seeking autonomy for Shaba

since Zaïre gained its independence from Belgium in 1960, launched a deadly strike on the region from their bases in Marxist-run Angola. [...] The rebels carried out cold-blooded executions, slaughtering at least 100 whites and 300 blacks, before they were driven from the city. [...]" (*Time*, p. 28, col. 1.)

Says Jalbert:

> "This report has a little more continuity, since the Katangese people are referred to as 'guerrillas' and 'rebels'." (285)

For the third time in less than two pages Jalbert equates the Katangan rebels with the Katangan people, and interprets categories applied to or actions attributed to the rebels as applied or attributed to the people. Especially in the context of the *Time* report, this distortion is utterly crude. Unlike *Newsweek*, *Time* magazine devotes a lot of attention to the identity of the rebels. They are described as mainly belonging to Lunda tribes. But the Lunda population (the 'people') of Shaba Province, who originally welcomed an earlier invasion in 1977, are now said to fear the rebels almost as much as Mobutu's repression. A Lunda contingent is said to have sought refuge in Zambia, just to be left alone. Thus a clear distinction is established between the rebels and the wider group of people to which they are related but who see themselves, in spite of a profound antipathy against Mobutu, as victims of the ongoing struggle. Be that as it may, the remark about the greater continuity established by using the categories 'guerrillas' and 'rebels', is completely beside the point. Not only is there no lack of continuity in *Newsweek's* categories 'rebels' and 'invaders' (to which this remark is an allusion). But the second, allegedly incongruent, category is also used throughout the *Time* article by referring to the reported event as an 'invasion' (already in the subtitle, conveniently left out of Jalbert's excerpt, "And the West once more helps Mobutu stop an invasion") or an 'incursion'.

An even more preposterous example of shallow analysis (if the term 'analysis' is still appropriate) follows:

> "These categories ['guerrillas' and 'rebels')], however, are juxtaposed with 'their bases in Marxist-run Angola'. The impression is given that Marxists condone 'cold-blooded executions' and the 'slaughtering' of people. There is also a subtle implication that a country espousing Marxism could not have a government, but could only be 'Marxist-run'." (285)

Let us look again at the first sentence of the excerpt, which is said to 'juxtapose' the category 'guerrillas' with 'their bases in Marxist-run Angola'. This sentence represents a remarkable feat of journalistic informativeness. It tells us who did something that was newsworthy, how many of them there were, what identifiable group they belong to, what the known goals of this group are, since when they have been operating, what they did, and where they came from. All this information is crucial for an understanding of the events reported, including the fact that the guerrillas have bases in the neighboring country Angola (which explains why they can get properly enough organized on a large enough scale to be able to launch a successful attack on Zaïrian territory) and the fact that Angola has a Marxist regime (which explains at least partly why Angola would want to provide shelter for a movement directed against a clearly anti-communist and dictatorial Mobutu). What boggles my mind is how the well-structured and informationally necessary 'juxtaposition' of the Katangese 'guerrillas' with 'their bases in Marxist-run Angola' could lead to the conclusion that the analyzed excerpt was designed to create the impression that Marxists, in general, condone 'cold-blooded executions' and the 'slaughtering' of people. It is my impression that only an oversensitive Marxist with an uneasy conscience could arrive at such a conclusion. To begin with, the analytical concept of 'juxtaposition' (just like 'reification' before) is misapplied (intentionally or not). The way Jalbert handles the notion (which basically means 'placing side by side') one could not predicate about the 'guerrillas' that they have 'bases in Marxist-run Angola' without 'juxtaposing' the category with the predicate. In other words, all information-carrying parts of a sentence, and of neighboring sentences (since 'rebels', the other 'juxtaposed' notion, does not occur until the next sentence), are 'juxtaposed' with each other. Nor does Jalbert stop at this level of trivializing the notion. His conclusion proceeds along a line of reasoning which we could call the Fallacy of the Touchy: for any blameworthy action A (in this case 'cold-blooded executions', 'slaughtering'), if A is ascribed to category X (the Katangese 'guerrillas'), and if category X is associated in any way with a wider category Y (Marxists) by means of any 'juxtaposed' information-carrying unit U ('their bases in Marxist-run Angola'), then every member of Y is implicitly accused of being an accomplice to A. Jalbert's indulgence in such fallacious reasoning is quite extreme, given the fact (blurred by his excerpting practices) that the information about the executions is separated from the guerrillas' 'bases in Marxist-run Angola' by another information-rich sentence which describes their major activity, the capture of Kolwezi:

> "In a seesaw battle with the forces of President Mobutu Sese Seko, the Katangese rebels — who variously refer to themselves as *les tigres* (French for tigers) or *camaradas* (Portuguese for comrades) — captured the provin-

cial capital of Kolwezi (pop. 100,000)." (*Time*, p. 28, col. 1.)

Throughout the article this is presented as the major event to be reported and explained, whereas the 'cold-blooded executions' and the 'slaughtering' of people are treated as a gruesome 'side effect'. No attempt is made to turn atrocities into typically Marxist practices. On the contrary, the terror of Mobutu's own regime is revealed in no uncertain terms:

> "In repelling last year's incursion, Mobutu's troops also behaved like soldiers — or worse. People suspected of helping the rebels were herded into huts, which were then doused with gasoline and set afire. Only the presence of the Moroccans, tribesmen say, prevented the death toll from rising into the thousands." (*Time*, p. 29, col. 3)

Rather than trying to create the impression that Marxists condone murder, the *Time* report makes it crystal-clear that the involvement of Western powers is motivated by a desire to safeguard their own sphere of influence in spite of the fact that "There are no lingering illusions in Washington, Paris or Brussels about the quality of Mobutu's regime." (*Time*, p. 30, col.1).

And what about Angola being 'Marxist-run'? Leaving aside the issue of the journalist's quite successful attempt to pack his sentence with a truckload of information, what else can be said about Jalbert's observation that there is "a subtle implication that a country espousing Marxism could not have a government, but could only be 'Marxist-run'"? Leaving aside yet another issue (concerned with the fact that, in English, *governments* can be said to *run* a country and that, by implication, 'Marxist-run' — when used attributively with the name of a country — simply *means* 'run by a Marxist government'), how can we test Jalbert's interpretation? Imagine that I believe that countries espousing Marxism could not have real governments. Could I convey this belief, with reference to the Soviet Union, by describing the Soviet Union as a 'Marxist-run' country? No. And why not? Because 'Marxist-run' carries a very different implication. The difference between 'Marxist countries' and 'Marxist-run countries' is that the latter implies '*presently* being run by a Marxist goverment'. The Soviet Union can only be described as a 'Marxist' country, since its Marxist form of government is viewed as highly stable and most kinds of social organization are thoroughly adapted to this fact. 'Marxist-run' is appropriate only to describe a recent state of affairs (for Angola: since 1976!) or one perceived as potentially subject to change. For analogous reasons one can talk about the 'Mobutu regime' to emphasize the personality-bound character (and possible transience) of the corresponding form of government, but not about the 'Reagan regime', because the Reagan administration is generally viewed as one instance of a long-standing political and governmental tradition. Generalizing the quite correct implication that Angola's Marxist government was not yet fully established or potentially unstable, to an underlying suggestion that no fully established or stable Marxist governments would be possible, is another one of Jalbert's analytical quirks.

The next sentence shows that Jalbert can hardly have read the articles:

> "We learn, however, that these Katangese people are members of the FINC [sic; see footnote 5], which grants them some political legitimacy, and seems to give them some purpose, in contrast with the *Newsweek* article, which gave us the impression that these people were 'invaders' who performed acts of violence for no justifiable reason." (285)

Also *Newsweek* identifies the Katangans as members of the Congolese National Liberation Front (p. 39, col. 2). So there is simply no factual basis for this comparative statement. The same is true for the 'invaders' category which, as said before, is equally perspicuous in *Time* magazine (and for which perfectly sufficient grounds can be adduced). As to the acts of violence, *Newsweek* does more than *Time* to exculpate the rebels' behavior by citing drinking (and possibly the taking of drugs) as one reason why an otherwise reasonable degree of discipline broke down. But both *Time* and *Newsweek* present some of the reported acts of violence, quite correctly, as atrocities for which there are indeed no justifiable reasons. And if Jalbert wants to tell us (as is implied in his criticism) that all those acts of violence can be exonerated, he should urgently demand a general revision of the definition of crimes of war, as specified by the Geneva conventions, ratified (though not necessarily observed) by a vast majority of the world's states.

"Even though the *Time* article attributes the invaders some purpose", Jalbert urges his readers to "consider another excerpt a little later in the same article" (285):

> "They insisted that no 'Cubanos' had come with them. Nonetheless, guerrillas declared that their goal was not simply the liberation of Shaba from Kinshasa's rule but the ouster of Mobutu and the creation of a more radical government in Zaïre." (*Time*, p. 29, col. 2.)

Jalbert's comment:

> "The word 'Nonetheless' implies that the Katangese people do not really have their *own* goals, that the goals they express are really Cuban goals, which implies further that the Katangese people are not capable of articulating such goals on their own." (285)

There would have been good reasons for this analysis, had the two sentences conjoined by 'nonetheless' not been taken out of their context. For one thing, what Jalbert calls 'a little later in the same article', as if nothing worth mentioning intervened, is in fact half-way through the article. This would not present a problem in itself. But in the paragraph preceding the one from which the two-sentence quotation was drawn, an attempt was made to trace the historical goals of the movement. The guerrillas are identified as Lundas, the tribesmen who wanted independence for Katanga under the leadership of the late Moïse Tshombé, "whose memory is still revered by many of the Angola-based rebels" (Time, p. 29, col. 2). The guerrillas now declare that they want to put an end to Mobutu's dictatorship for Zaïre as a whole. This shift from an (originally right-wing) independence movement to a left-wing liberation movement, certainly calls for an explanation. Especially given the continued reverence for Moïse Tshombé, it is natural to ask whether the rebels have indeed changed their basic goals, or whether new circumstances dictate them to voice aims more in line with the Marxist ideology of their host country Angola and their Cuban advisers. In the light of such a question, the implication carried by 'nonetheless' is *exactly the opposite* of what Jalbert reads in it: since the rebels do not need Cuban companions to voice their wider goal, nor to try to achieve it, the goal in question may indeed have become their *own*. The question of whether the shift results from opportunistic adaptability or not, is left open. If that is what Jalbert wants to criticize, he should pronounce a ban on speculation about people's motives. But then all attempts at interpretive reporting and, for that matter, all interesting approaches to social science would effectively terminate.

The foregoing considerations, which could be multiplied by commenting on just about any other sentence in "Some constructs for analysing news", lead us to the somewhat shocking conclusion that 'detailed analyses' by scholars such as Paul L. Jalbert show more traces of ideological bias than the media they want to crucify for lack of 'objectivity'. Is scholarship not supposed to be more objective than a news report which can be shown to be subject to all kinds of social constraints (see chapter 1)? Paradoxically, whereas the presence of such constraints necessarily diminishes the level of 'objectivity' of the mass media, their near-absence in the case of academic writing seems to enable scholars to disregard demands for objectivity almost completely. Hardly anyone outside the academic community will get to see Jalbert's article. Of those insiders who get to see it, most will not read it. Of the remaining minority, most will quickly glance through it. Of those who really begin to read it, some will find that it confirms their own beliefs (in which case — following an Orwellian maxim — they may keep reading and they may even find an occasion or two to refer to the article in their own writings), and some will disagree (in which case they are likely to stop after a few pages and to put it out of their minds forever). Getting criticized at length is simply Jalbert's bad luck. Such absence of expected social monitoring and sanctioning (rarely ameliorated by editorial scrutiny) enables one to present even the wildest speculations as factual accounts yielding profound insights. Since the use of this opportunity is often enjoyed to the fullest, it is just as well that there is not a wider readership for products of scholarship.

2.2. Like-minded judges

Why was so much time and space devoted to comments on an article the usefulness of which was plainly renounced? For two conjoined reasons. First, though it is an extreme example, Paul L. Jalbert's "Some constructs for analysing news" is rather representative for linguistic studies of the news media. Second, this state of affairs is quite alarming and something should be done to upgrade the quality of research, given the centrality of linguistic issues in communicative approaches to the media. In this section, we offer two more illustrations to substantiate the first of these claims. In the final section of this chapter, before presenting a brief case study, some relevant questions will be reviewed.

In "Death of a premier: Consensus and closure in international news", Howard Davis and Paul Walton (1983) comment on the reporting (in Britain, Germany, and the USA) of the Aldo Moro kidnapping and murder case in 1978. They focus on television news, but also include references to newspapers in their analysis. Their accusatory conclusion has already been mentioned (see section 2.0). But it is worth looking into the details which lead them to the insight (which should be regarded as a predictable property of mass media reports rather than a hidden fact to be discovered) that the reports reflect some kind of ideological 'consensus' (or, in our terms, are anchored in a common ground for communication). The other side of consensus is said to be 'closure', the exclusion of diverging points of view. Davis and Walton's analysis concentrates on ways of achieving such closure, or on techniques of exclusion.

> "In the German press, for instance, but not regularly elsewhere, the term 'Red Brigades' was nearly always surrounded by inverted commas. The term 'self-styled' occurred several times in the English-language press. The broadcast equivalent used several times was the prefix 'so-called'. It was a

premise of almost all this reporting that the Red Brigades were a very small group without political status which commanded little support from the Italian people.

The second linguistic technique of exclusion is one which places the Red Brigades outside 'normal' society by the application of heavily value-laden labels and stereotypes. 'Criminal' was one such label used, together with kindred terms like 'killers', 'gunmen' and 'murderers'. [...]

Another group of terms is derived from *military* and *political* vocabularies and they are frequently used in combination. There were references to 'guerrillas' or 'urban guerrillas' [...]; 'commandos' [...]; 'a guerrilla squad' and 'a highly organized guerrilla army' [...]. The political descriptions most frequently invoke the left/right continuum, extremism and revolution, with references to 'left-wing', 'extremist', or both. [...]

A third interpretive category is used more widely in the press than in broadcast news. It assumes the *psychopathological* nature of the Red Brigades' activities [...]. Newspapers employed such terms as 'fanatics' [...], 'crazies' [...], 'evil-minded children' [...]. The broadcasters appeared to avoid specific use of a psychopathological model but were working with similar assumptions when they referred to the Red Brigades' 'latest macabre trick' (BBC) and 'sadistic torments' (ZDF). [...]

Each of the models of interpretation described here (the criminal, military, political and psychopathological) can of course be applied to other quite distinct groups and activities. The significance of their conjunction in the Moro story is to provide multiple guarantees of the Red Brigades' exclusion from the membership categories of the audience — 'the overwhelming majority', 'the people', 'ordinary citizens'. These inclusive categories are widely used in descriptions of the public shock, outrage and sorrow which followed the news of Moro's death. Linguistically, they express the consensus from which the Red Brigades are excluded by the means described above." (40-41)

After a few additional remarks, grudgingly admitting that the media do not always present the consensus as complete, and hastily comparing the 'distancing devices' of the Moro story with those discovered in earlier research on industrial disputes (see Glasgow University Media Group 1980), they sharpen their indictment:

"In the present case, where impartiality is not sought, the real significance of the patterns of language which we have noted appears to lie in the 'ideological work' which is routinely performed at the boundaries of *inclusion* and *exclusion*." (43)

In other words, the media are explicitly accused of being tendentious and of making it impossible for members of their audience to identify themselves with the Red Brigades.

Even assuming that their data are presented accurately (unlike in Jalbert's case), the conclusions in this article are clearly the result of preconceived notions about what *ought* to be 'discovered' rather than of significant research questions designed to test a hypothesis. A crucial question, which does not come up in Davis and Walton's discussion, is the following: What is the degree of accuracy with which the way in which the media depicted the Red Brigades corresponds to what reporters knew (or could reasonably be expected to have known)? For instance, would it be objectionable or tendentious to describe the Red Brigades as "a very small group without political status which commanded little support from the Italian people"? As to the 'small group', whether it was 'very small' (as they say is implied in the use of inverted commas, and the expressions 'self-styled' and 'so-called') or 'relatively small' (as they explicitly say themselves; p. 48), does not seem to be a serious matter for dispute. Are the Red Brigades 'without political status'? Of course they are. Not because the *media* exclude them from participation in regular political life. They are *self-excluding* in their refusal to abide by the rules governing political conduct in an established democratic society, however imperfect it may be. They are self-excluding in their open defiance, not only of political rules, but even of the generally accepted (though, unfortunately, not always honored) humanitarian laws of war. Thus it is even factually correct to depict them as a group standing "outside 'normal' society" and to apply "heavily value-laden labels" to them by defining them as 'criminals'. As to the 'little support from the Italian people', again this probably reflects a basic truth. Essentially, terrorism is the weapon of the weak. In dictatorial regimes, as in Latin America, this weakness results from the repressive machinery put into action by the politically powerful. But in democratic nations (where, whatever terrorists may say, there are always ways of promoting change without resorting to murder) weakness is another word for lack of support. The label 'fanatics' seems quite appropriate for those who, in the fact of insufficient public support, have recourse to terrorist tactics to achieve their goals. Paradoxically, the use of such tactics "only serves to isolate them further and to alienate potential support" (P. Wilkinson 1979: 133). (This mechanism is also at work in the international arena where, for instance, the PLO's shift away from terrorist practices was motivated by, and exerted a significant influence on, their growing recognition in the 1970's as representatives of the Palestinian people.) Finally, the military and political vocabularies used to talk about the Red Brigades are hardly media inventions serving the cause of 'exclusion'. If they act like an 'urban guerrilla army', why should such a phrase be shunned? If they show themselves to be 'extremists', the media are not at fault for using the term. And if they characterize their own goals as 'left-wing', any account avoiding this attribute would be incomplete.

Any trial which disregards reflections of this kind is a circus trial. Sadly enough, Davis and Walton's analysis tells us more about their own biases than about the media's handling of the Moro news story about which they claim that it "tells more about the maintenance of an ideologically safe version of consensus [...] than it does about the 'events' which constitute the news" (48).

A final, equally discouraging, example of a linguistic analysis of the media's performance is drawn from Gunther Kress's "Linguistic and ideological transformations in news reporting" (1983). In one section of this article, Kress analyzes the use of verbs as opposed to nominalizations in the first three sentences from two newspaper texts (one from the Adelaide afternoon paper the *News*, the other from the Melbourne morning paper the *Age*), both dealing with an impending strike by telecommunications technicians. The *Age* extract:

> "*Industrial disputes*
> TELECOM STRIKE THREAT
> 1. Telecom employees are likely to reimpose work bans or strike within a week unless their demands are met on pay negotiations.
> 2. The federal executive of the 26,000-member Australian Telecommunications Employees Association drew up a plan for a fresh industrial campaign after a seven-hour meeting yesterday.
> 3. The recommendations will be put to members in Sydney today, in Brisbane, Perth, Adelaide and Hobart tomorrow, and in Melbourne next Tuesday."

The *News* excerpt:

> "PHONE CHAOS LIKELY NEXT WEEK
> TV strike continues
> 1. Industrial action seems certain to hit the nation's telecommunications network from early next week.
> 2. Effects will be felt in South Australia — where more than 2500 Telecom workers will meet tomorrow.
> 3. Most likely action is bans on new business phone installations, bans on maintenance and bans on repairs to call-recording equipment."

Neither the restrictedness of the corpus, nor the narrowness of the topic (verbs *vs.* nominalizations — where Kress especially emphasizes the fact that nominalizations often enable a reporter to avoid mentioning exactly who is involved in the events and activities reported), can prevent the formulation of the following sweeping conclusion:

> "The pattern is clear [...]. Both reporters use a specific ideological grid which they impose on the events. In the case of the *Age* it is a broadly pluralist ideology of industrial relations (as well as specific views of the function of management, including 'union management'); in the case of the *News* it is an ideology of essential conflict, less a model of industrial relations than of class struggle. The two ideologies determine the reporting of the event, that is, they structure the linguistic interpretation of the event. In the one case the (nominal) categories of one kind of industrial relations theory are imposed on the world. Within this model most processes are absorbed into abstract nominal concepts. [...] In the other case highly abstract categories of contention and conflict at the largest social level are imposed on the same world." (134)

Accepting the rather wild assumption that such a conclusion could reasonably be drawn on the basis of a narrowly focused look at a minuscule 'corpus', one would at least hope that this 'look' would be a detailed in-depth analysis. However, only some furtive comments are made on each of the six sentences investigated. Take, for instance, the commentary on sentence 2 from the *News*:

> "Sentence 2, the *News*: 'Effects will be felt in South Australia — where more than 2500 Telecom workers will meet tomorrow.' The verbs are: '(will be) felt', '(will) meet'; the nominalizations: 'effects', 'workers'. The 'experiencer' of 'felt' is not given (it is the deleted subject of the passive), though there is a 'surrogate' experiencer, 'in South Australia'. That is, rather than naming the people or institutions who will be affected, the reporter suggests that it will be 'felt (by everyone) in South Australia'. This was patently not the case, though given the paradigm which the reporter has invoked in the first sentence and which is continued here, it is a necessary linguistic and ideological device for him to use. *Effect*, like *action* [commented on by Kress in connection with the 'industrial action' of the first sentence], is difficult to decode with any degree of accuracy: it is not clear precisely what will affect precisely whom." (133)

Does the reporter really suggest that the effects of the impending industrial action will be felt by *everyone* in South Australia? That 'this was patently not the case' is easy to say with the benefit of hindsight. But even when disregarding this element of unfairness in Kress's judgment, his interpretation is seriously warped. A regular reader would not interpret the sentence as a prediction that *everyone* in South Australia *would* be affected, but as a simple statement that *everyone depending in Telecom services* in South Australia *could* potentially feel the effects of the expected industrial action. No reasonable reader would assume, at that point in time, the reporter to have been in a position 'to name the people or institutions' that would be affected. But to top it all off, Kress completely ignores that the very next sentence (which even belongs to his 'corpus'!) specifies exactly what services were most likely to be suspended. This not only narrows down the range of interpretations for 'effect', but it also gives a quite concrete form to the types of 'industrial action' to be undertaken. Hence the specification of what will be done or what will affect whom, rather than being drowned in the vagueness of 'highly abstract categories', is as precise as could reasonably be expected of a non-clairvoyant reporter. Briefly, Kress's verdict that the reporting is guided by ideological bias rather than by the available information is clearly, whether he knows it or not, a blow below the belt.

2.3 Relevant questions

If the foregoing commentaries have created the impression that it is this author's intention to exculpate those responsible for news reporting of every possible charge, it is high time to set the record straight. And if an indiscriminate rejection of *all* linguistic studies of the media has been read into them, it is also urgent to prevent this interpretation from taking root.

A treasure of pertinent observations, not just on the use of language in news reporting, but on matters of 'an ecology of language' in general, is to be found in Dwight Bolinger's *Language — The Loaded Weapon* (1980) and spread out over many of his other publications. But Bolinger is the conspicuous exception whose authority is thoroughly abused by many others. Some of his apt remarks are even quoted by Paul L. Jalbert (1983: 288):

> "Bombing is 'protective reaction', precision bombing is 'surgical strikes', concentration camps are 'pacification centers' or 'refugee camps' ... Bombs dropped outside the target area are 'incontinent ordnance', and those dropped on one of your own villages are excused as 'friendly fire'; a bombed house becomes automatically a 'military structure' and a lowly sampan sunk on the waterfront a 'waterborne logistic craft'." (Bolinger 1973: 545)

The origin of these euphemisms is the U.S. government's news management (by way of press releases, communiqués, press conferences, etc.) during the Vietnam war. The media are to blame to the extent of their unreflecting adoption of the official language camouflaging a cruel and unjust reality. But little does Jalbert realize that this criticism is the best argument possible to justify the use of clearly value-laden terminologies. Yet the use of such a terminology in the *Time* and *Newsweek* coverage of events in Zaïre was denounced as ideological manipulation. In this case, Jalbert would have preferred euphemisms. Whether the culprits are American soldiers, Katangan rebels or, for that matter, Italy's Red Brigades, atrocities should be presented as atrocities. That is the real message in Bolinger's comment.

The linguistic literature does not only present us with Bolinger-type investigations of aspects of language use, applied or immediately applicable to the language of the news media. Other relevant studies are conducted within the framework of more or less rigidly defined paradigms of research, such as ethnomethodology. To give just one example, Jim Schenkein's "The radio raiders story" (1979) is a detailed consideration — though only with reference to one example — of the methods newspapers routinely use to transform stories about events 'in the world' into stories 'in the news'. This is not a trivial issue. Schenkein shows how it touches upon the use a newspaper can make of an already existing relationship between the reader and 'the news' (taking into account the structural properties of news reporting, some of which were sketched in chapter 1), and how it involves the step-by-step piecing together of bits of information and the ordering of a variety of perspectives on essentially identical pieces of information to gradually compose a picture of the events reported and the participants involved.

In addition to such investigations, various useful lines of research are possible. For instance, capitalizing on the simple fact that all reporting necessarily presupposes and defines a common ground — ideologically and otherwise — one could embark on detailed investigations of the very substance of the world view which a newspaper (or magazine, or television network) assumes it shares with its readership (or audience). All conceptual tools which linguistic pragmatics has made available for the analysis of implicit meaning, could be put to use in this context.

A quite different topic, essential to the study of international news reporting, would be to trace the 'communicative history' of news items. This history starts with events abroad, possibly mediated by eye-witness accounts or reports in the local press, (re)told in reports by foreign correspondents and/or the international news agencies, adapted to the needs of the major national newspapers, and possibly further filtered out for use in secondary papers (without their own 'direct' sources). At each of these stages one might observe the loss of contextualization cues or the addition of new, culture-specific, presuppositions. The effect of such natural communication processes on the shaping of the picture of the events as it reaches its widest audience, could then be stated with a high degree of precision and accuracy.

None of these questions, however, can be approached sensibly from a purely linguistic point of view. A large amount of real-world knowledge has to be gathered and taken into account at all times. Not only is familiarity with the structure of news reporting practices (as briefly outlined in chapter 1) required. Adequate information about the reported events is also indispensable. Otherwise one cannot hope to answer the question (pointed out as crucial in section 2.2) as to the degree of accuracy with which the way events are presented corresponds to what reporters and staff writers knew or could reasonably be expected to have known. But any adequate answer to such a question also calls for knowledge about those reporters (and staff writers). Who were they? What was their background? How familiar were they with the culture, customs, language of the society in which the reported events took place? On what grounds were they selected for the job? On what grounds did they accept? Or did they not have any choice? In other words, the approach has to be profoundly pragmatic. As a consequence, interdisciplinary cooperation is vital to the entire enterprise.

3. A CASE STUDY: THE TOPIC

3.0. Introduction: The U-2 incident

As we have demonstrated (in section 2.3), it is not difficult to ask relevant questions of a wide-ranging nature about the processes and practices of international news reporting, to the answering of which linguistic research can make a significant contribution. What is more problematic is to single out a restricted topic for a case study in such a way as to preserve maximum relevance in relation to the wider issues.

A first requirement seems to be that the event, the reporting of which is to be investigated, should carry clear international significance. Further, the event should be far enough in the past, so that a proper perspective is readily available on what really happened. To satisfy both of these conditions, we have selected as a corpus all *The New York Times* reports (from Friday, May 6th to Friday, May 20th, 1960) concerning the shooting down, over Soviet territory, of an American U-2 spy plane on May 1st, and its effects on the East-West Summit Conference held in Paris later that month.

Such a corpus, however restricted it may be, still requires a further focusing of analytical attention. The problem is, then, what the most promising center of interest could be. The downing of the U-2 was not just a military feat for the Russians, nor a simple setback for the U.S. spying program. Almost immediately it developed into a major political incident, that is, into a basically communicative event. Since the media did not have direct access to the 'event', the reporting necessarily centered around what the various parties involved (especially Soviet and American government officials, including Nikita Khrushchev and Dwight Eisenhower) had to say about it, both to each other and to the press. Thus an interesting focus could be the way in which *The New York Times* reports present the communicative behavior of the protagonists, the use of language shaping the incident. This would lead us to a meta-level of analysis (already hinted at in section 2.0) usually ignored in linguistic studies of the media.

To clarify the methodological framework, this chapter will briefly sketch (in section 3.1) some basic properties of metapragmatic terms, i.e. natural language terms used to describe verbal behavior. And the special significance, with reference to our topic, of further focusing on metapragmatic metaphors, will be explained (in section 3.2).

3.1. Metapragmatic terms

Central to the set of devices available to speakers of English for the description of *activities* or forms of behavior, is the repertoire of verbs and verb-like expressions (or *verbials*[6]). Applied to our topic, the most prominent set of *metapragmatic terms* in English is the inventory of *linguistic action verbials*, i.e. the verbs and verb-like expressions used to describe (aspects of) *linguistic action*. The basic properties of linguistic action verbials (LAVs) have to be reviewed briefly before their functioning in our newspaper corpus can be investigated.[7]

To begin with, one should realize that any analysis of LAVs involves using language to describe language used in the description of language. This double layering adds to the risk of circularity haunting inquiries into any lexical domain. A non-circular analysis of LAVs should specify the conditions under which a verb V can be appropriately used in a description D of a linguistic action A. Those conditions can be formulated as conditions on or properties of the act to be described (A) and sometimes in terms of conditions on or properties of the describing act (D). These conditions or properties (C) may be symbolized as 'C' if they bear on A, and as 'Cd' if they bear on D.

Taking into account the various objects and levels of adaptation involved in any speech event[8], both A and D involve at least the following elements with reference to which semantic dimensions can be specified along which the meanings of LAVs vary: both A and D are performed within the setting of a physical and social 'objective' world; both involve a speaker/author or speakers/authors, symbolized by Sa in the former case and Sd in the latter, and a hearer/reader or hearers/readers, symbolized as Ha for A and Hd for D; between Sa and Ha, and Sd and Hd, and often between all of them, there are certain social relationships; individually, Sa, Ha, Sd and Hd all have their beliefs, desires, intentions; Sa and Sd also have, more specifically, communicative intentions which they act upon linguistically to score certain communicative effects in Ha and Hd; this linguistic 'acting upon' their communicative intentions consists in Sa's and Sd's making of a large number of linguistic choices; those linguistic choices can be situated at all or any of the levels of linguistic structuring which are 'adaptable' (including at least: language, code, channel, communication type, style, text, speech act, propositional content, sentence structure, phrase, word, morpheme, phoneme, sound features).

The conditions which have to be formulated to account for the meaning of LAVs can be attached to any of the constitutive elements of A or D mentioned. They are always points on some semantic dimension characterizing one, or a combination of, these elements. Figure 1 visualizes this descriptive framework.

For the present purposes, one illustration should be sufficient to demonstrate how semantic dimensions, and hence conditions-of-use, can be formulated with reference to the elements presented in Figure 1. Consider the English verb *to lie*. Its prototypically appropriate use in a description D of an utterance act A requires:

(i) that the propositional content of Sa's utterance deviates from a true state of affairs;
(ii) that Sa believes that what is expressed in the propositional content of his utterance deviates from a true state of affairs;
(iii) that Sa intends to deceive Ha.

(i) specifies one pole on a truth-falsity dimension attached to choices made at the propositional content level. (ii) determines a value on a sincerity dimension related to Sa's world of beliefs. (iii) makes a selection from a wide range of possible communicative intentions on the part of Sa.

All these conditions are attached to elements of A; they could be called A-conditions. But the use of *to lie* often involves D-conditions as well. Not only are (i), (ii) and (iii) reflected in D as beliefs held by Sd, the one who selects *to lie* for use in his description D of utterance act A. There is also at least one condition that can only be specified with reference to D. Typically, Sd will not use *to lie* unless he wants to pass a negative moral judgment on what Sa did. And a decision to do so will partly depend on Sd's evaluation of the graveness of the consequences, in terms of the communicative effect on Ha. How this general profile of *to lie* (more details of which should be specified if the example did not serve a purely illustrative purpose) relates to our descriptive framework, is presented in Figure 2.

So far, we have only exemplified usage conditions defining the prototypical meaning of LAVs.[9] In discussing actual usage, it is no longer appropriate to specify 'conditions' of use but only to describe meaningful 'properties' of use. These may deviate in various ways from the prototypical conditions. Or

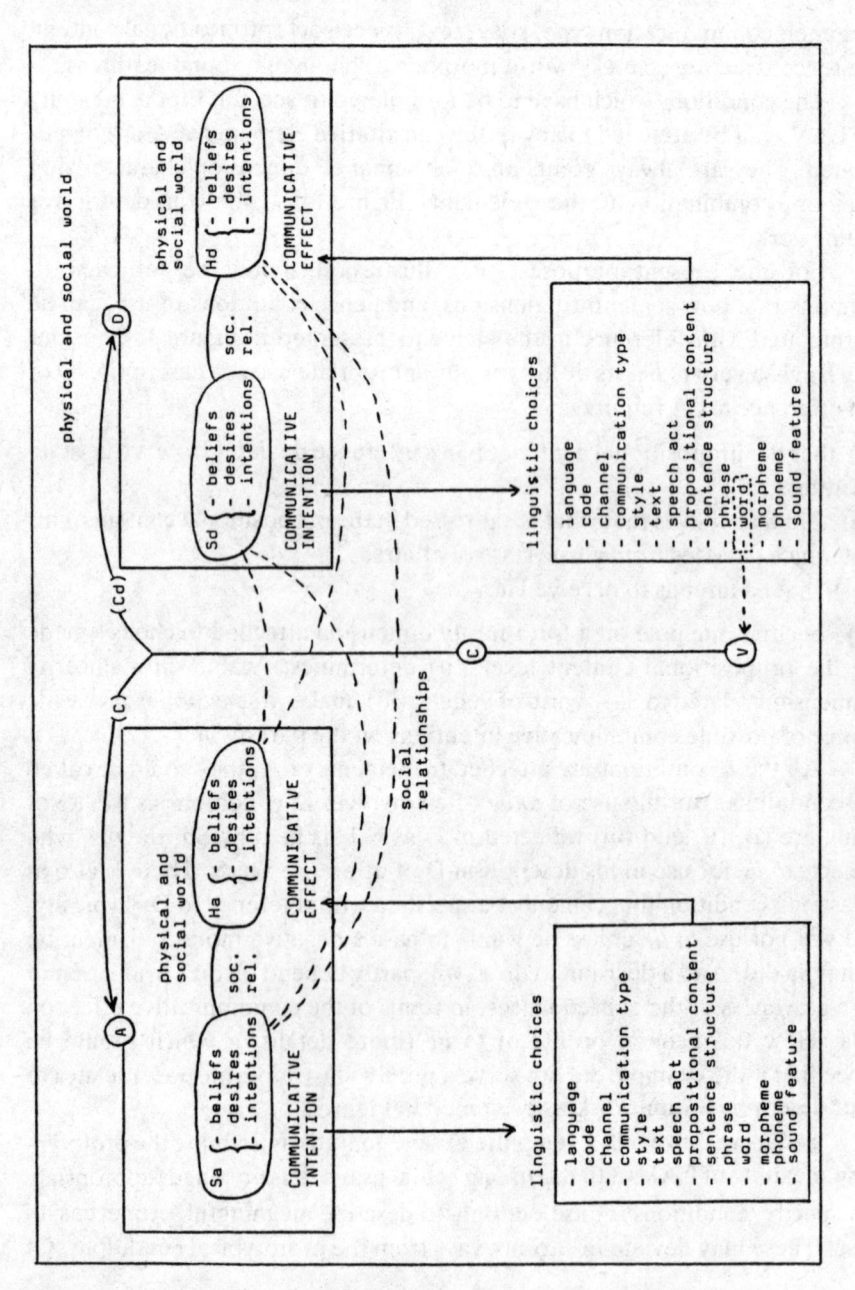

Figure 1. Descriptive framework

THE TOPIC

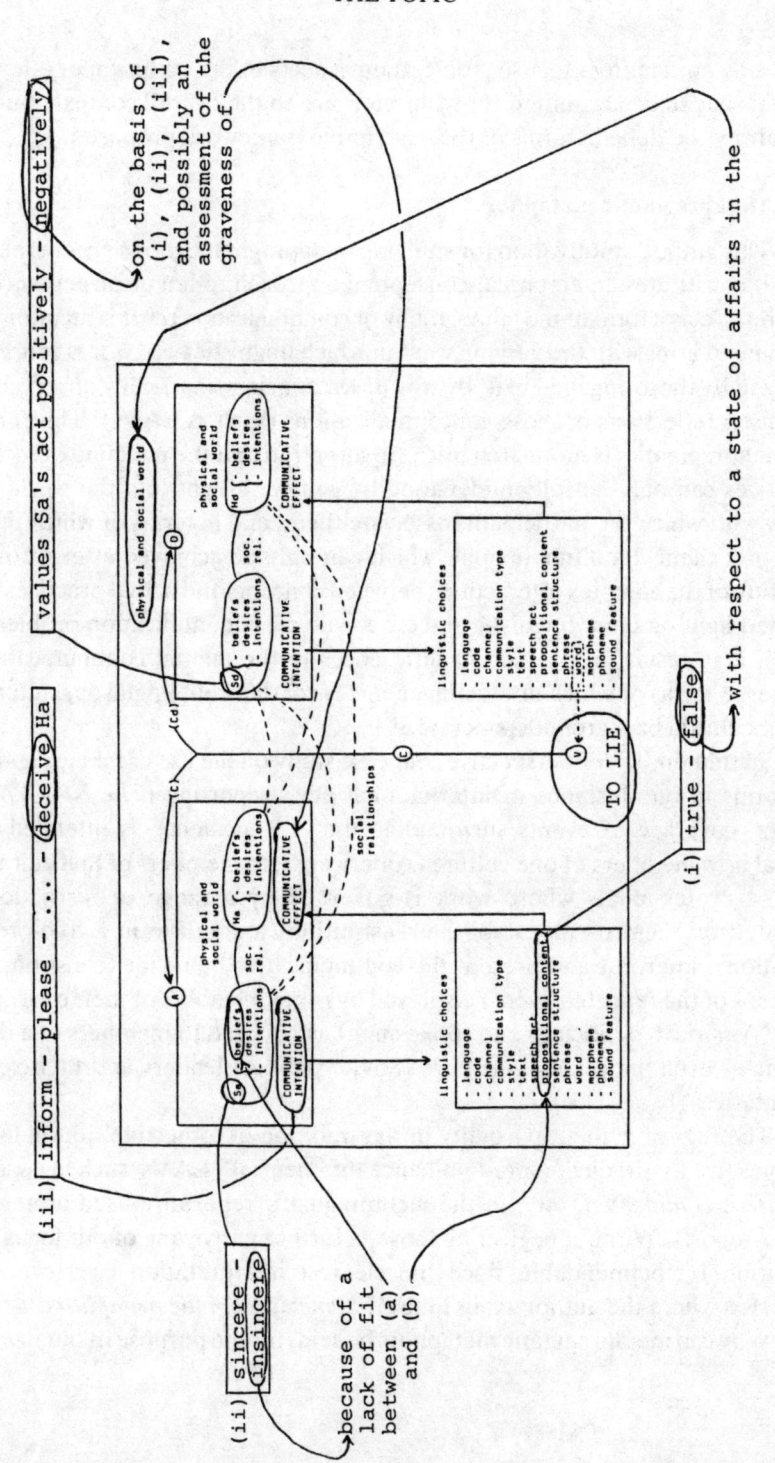

Figure 2. Profile of _to lie_

they may amount to a focusing on certain aspects to the exclusion of others. All this has to be accounted for with reference to the overall context. But it can always be done in terms of the descriptive framework proposed.

3.2. Metapragmatic metaphors

This author's motivation for studying metapragmatic terms in general, is that it constitutes an empirical-conceptual approach to linguistic action (interpretable as a form of the ethnography of communication).[10] It is an attempt to come to grips with the varying ways in which linguistic behavior is conceptualized by those engaged in it, by way of scrutinizing empirically observable linguistic reflections of those conceptualizations (such as LAVs). This form of metapragmatics is motivated by the assumption that the meaning of social practices can only be fully understood by gaining insight into the world of ideas with which the participants associate them, and in terms of which they interpret them. Its ultimate goal, which can only be achieved after further scrutiny of the complex interactions between concepts and actual practices, is to shed light on cross-linguistic and cross-cultural communication problems which may result, in part, from differences in the mental communicative frames in terms of which interacting members of different linguistic, cultural or subcultural backgrounds, operate.[11]

Within this wider perspective, our case study on the use of metapragmatic terms in one instance of international news reporting (*The New York Times'* coverage of events surrounding the U-2 incident), is intended to reveal how members of one culture (Americans), as members of that culture and as professionals whose work is governed by a range of restrictions imposed on them by an established institution (journalism in a free-press tradition), interpret and present the communicative behavior (constituting the core of the reported event) displayed by other members of their own culture (American politicians and spokesmen) as opposed to members of a different — even antipodal — culture (Soviet political leaders and their representatives).

The fear of evident partiality in the tradition of 'objective' journalism enables us to predict a predominance of 'neutral' LAVs such as *said*, *declared*, *commented*, etc., in the metapragmatic repertoire used in newspaper reports. Without neglecting those, a further narrowing of our focus of attention is commendable since the clearest interpretation cues can be expected where the author avails himself of *metapragmatic metaphors*.

Why can metapragmatic metaphors be said, for the purpose of our investigation, to present clearer interpretation cues than most 'neutral' LAVs? Because metaphors highlight a particular point on a particular dimension of variation (or semantic dimension) in terms of which the activity described could be conceived. Thus a stock metaphor such as *to get across to someone* emphasizes the dimension of message transfer (seen in 'spatial' terms), whereas *to put something into words* singles out the dimension of encoding (viewed in terms of a 'container').[12] Even dead metaphors, as in *to speak out*, bring a particular dimension into focus, in this case the source from which a message is supposed to emanate (again described in 'spatial' terms). In this way, the set of metapragmatic metaphors in current use in a language community highlights fundamental facts about the conception of linguistic activity in terms of which the members of that community interact and perceive verbal interaction.

To get a clear idea of such basic aspects of the relationship between the metaphorical lexicalization of linguistic action and its conceptualization, a complete survey (preferably even comparing several languages spoken in markedly distinct cultures or subcultures) is required. Otherwise a proper assessment of the relative importance of various metaphors is out of the question, so that there is an imminent danger of misleading conclusions. Similarly, exhaustiveness has to be approached in the following investigation of a concrete corpus, if we hope to establish the functional link between the context of the metapragmatic descriptions (including the 'real-world' event, the goals of the reporters, properties of the audience, etc.) and the metaphors chosen for the description.

3.3. The topic

Recapitulating briefly, our case study consists of a linguistic description of the metapragmatic notions handled in *The New York Times* to account for the communicative events constituting the U-2 incident. Special attention will be paid to the functioning of metapragmatic metaphors.

In the next chapter, the complete set of data will be presented, with comments, for the first three days of reporting. This will clarify the basic pattern of the functional distribution of metapragmatic description types, enabling us to comentt more selectively on the remainder of the corpus. The final chapter will be devoted to a further analysis and conclusions.

4. A CASE STUDY: DATA AND COMMENTS

4.0. Introduction

With Figure 1 in mind, it is easy to present a brief overview of the crucial elements involved in the reporting (D) and in the reported political-communicative event (A). Both the communicative and the meta-communicative events are situated in a common historical context. The year is 1960. The date of the first reports is May 6th. An event, confronting the world's two most powerful nations with each other, had happened almost a week before, on May 1st. A plane was shot down over Soviet territory. This did not lead to any confrontation until Soviet authorities announced the event, adding that the plane was American, and that it was on a spying mission. The wider context is one in which significant improvements in U.S.-Soviet relations were noticeable. In September 1959, Khrushchev had visited Washington. He had taken a personal liking to President Eisenhower. He had seen with his own eyes — particularly impressed by the high standard of living — that a capitalist country was not necessarily such a hell after all. And he was more convinced than ever that peaceful coexistence was possible (though he could not refrain from announcing to the Americans that their grandchildren would live under communism). Consequently, not only Khrushchev, but also Eisenhower and other western leaders (particularly British prime minister Harold Macmillan) had high hopes for a four-power summit meeting which was to be held in Paris (barely two weeks after the downing of the plane) — in spite of the thorny Berlin issue on the agenda. In addition, Eisenhower had been invited to pay a return visit to Moscow in June.

So much for the historical context. Let us have a brief look now at the participants in A and D. Sa is always Khrushchev or Eisenhower or a representative of their governments. However, our knowledge of political life tells us that the Sa involved is not comparable to a regular speaker in an everyday conversation. On the American side, a network of advisers is usually consulted before the President issues an official statement. And if a spokesman does the talking, he may simply have been instructed to say what he is saying. On the Soviet side, official announcements can be assumed to have been approved or inspired by a majority of Politburo members. The structure of Ha is equally complex. The Sa's mentioned direct their utterances at each other or at people from the press. But through those Ha's, also the wider audience of the international community is aimed at. The inevitable presence of this more general Ha constrains what Sa can say. In a sense, the communicative intentions of the various Sa's may focus less on scoring communicative effects in each other than on influencing the general public, not only on the American side (where public opinion is of immediate political concern) but also on the Soviet side (where different motivations underlie the maintenance of an extensive propaganda machine). As to Sa's linguistic choices, particularly the choice of language may be relevant in interpreting the reported communicative exchanges. At least certain aspects of these exchanges and of their reporting may be explicable in terms of the differences between English and Russian. Unfortunately, we are not in a position to go into those issues within the context of this case study.

As to the describing act D, Sd is always a reporter or commentator affiliated with *The New York Times*. Their communicative intention is the giving of 'objective' information, within the confines of a free press tradition of international news reporting (as discussed in Chapter 1). In fact, all Sd's function as a subset of the instruments through which the various Sa's try to reach their widest range of Ha's indirectly — the general public or the international community. Hd, constituting a subset of indirectly addressed Ha's, is the general readership of *The New York Times*, which can be safely assumed to be thoroughly familiar with the historical context sketched above.

Our topic of investigation concerns Sd's choices, at the word (or lexical item) level, from the set of metapragmatic verbials to describe A. These choices are functionally related to the overall context of A and D, but also to linguistic choices made at different levels of structure. They are related to the choice of a stylistic level of formality or informality; to the norms of the chosen communication type, 'news reporting', itself; to the limitations imposed or possibilities opened by using the channel of writing; to the conventions of journalistic and political jargon at the code level. And in view of the fact that about half of the reporting under investigation is about communication in Russian, the inevitable choice of English as the language of the reporting may have relevant consequences. Studying this cross-linguistic and cross-cultural translation and interpretation problem would require a vast amount of additional data (such as the precise Russian texts and utterances that constitute the subject of the news) and extensive preliminary research (such as a comparative survey of English and Russian lexicalized concepts of verbal behavior). Any speculations about this will therefore be treated as outside the scope of the present study. In our comments on the data (this chapter) and in the further analysis and conclusions (in Chapter 5), however, an attempt will be made to keep in mind all other functional interrelations between levels of linguistic structuring involved in D.

The basic framework in terms of which our corpus can be approached, is schematized in Figure 3. This sketch only presents a static skeleton of an extremely dynamic complex of organisms. For one thing, the beliefs held by Hd about Sd's beliefs about the events as seen by the various Sa's (and about the various Sa's beliefs about each other's beliefs) are in constant flux and have to be adapted to every newly available piece of information. Note that Hd's and Sd's beliefs do not necessarily coincide: every educated Hd knows that Sd can only reveal his beliefs under certain institutionally determined conditions (one of them being a high degree of certainly about their correctness). When presenting the corpus in the following sections, summaries will be provided for articles from which metapragmatically relevant sentences (with reference to the U-2) have been excerpted (either per article or per day), in order to enable the reader to fill out the constantly changing details of the framework for himself.

Every excerpted sentence in the corpus will be coded with reference to the following parameters:

(i) The source of the reported verbal behavior: American (U.S.) or Soviet (U.S.S.R.); if Amercan, Eisenhower (E) or someone else (others); if Soviet, Khrushchev (K) or someone else (others).
(ii) The mode in which the content of the reported utterance(s) is presented: full quotation (Q); semi-quote (sQ), i.e. with only a word or a phrase between quotation marks; or simply reported speech (R).
(iii) The metaphorical status of the (italicized) metapragmatic terms and expressions: non-metaphorical (nM) or metaphorical (M); and if metaphorical, dead metaphor (dM), or stock metaphor (sM). Note that creative metaphors (cM) hardly occur at all.

Diagrams presenting the distribution of metapragmatic description types along these parameters will be offered for the first three, fully documented, days of reporting (giving figures for all articles individually). Though these data are basically statistic (so that they cannot form the basis for an interpretative analysis), the parameters introduce distinctions which will help us

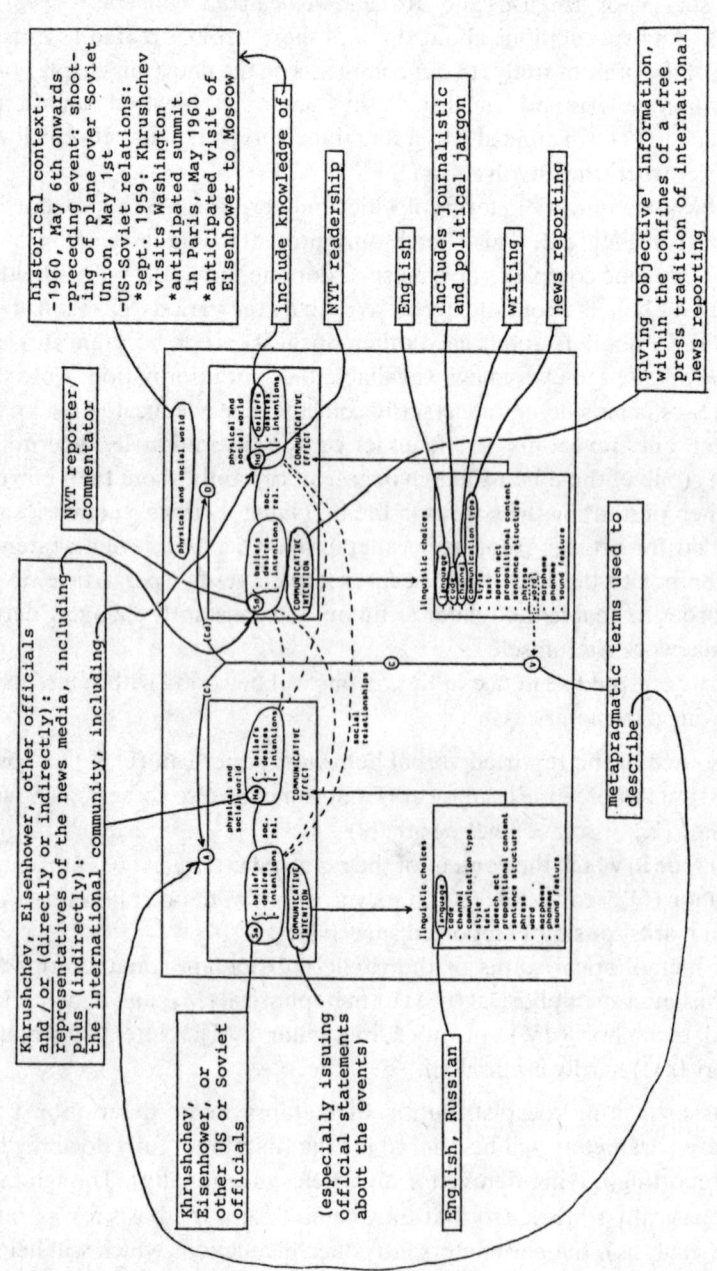

Figure 3. General framework for the NYT corpus

to avoid formulating misleading generalized conclusions.

4.1. May 6th

4.1.1. *Article 1 (front page)*

TITLE: Soviet downs American plane; U.S. *says* it was weather craft; Khrushchev sees summit blow. [U.S.: others/R/nM]
(Note: this title covers both article 1 and article 2, presenting the U.S. and Soviet versions of the event, respectively, and written by two different reporters.)
SUBTITLE: Capital *explains*. [U.S.: others/R/nM]
SUB-SUBTITLE: *Reports* unarmed U-2 vanishes at border after difficulty. [U.S.: others/R/nM]
AUTHOR: Jack Raymond
CONTENTS: A NASA statement is quoted as saying that a weather-observation plane, piloted by a civilian, Francis G. Powers, had been missing since Sunday, May 1st. Details are given about the type of plane, a U-2 high-altitude one-man craft powered by a single turbojet engine, built by Lockheed for the Air Force to study radioactivity resulting from nuclear tests, but also being used for weather observation. Details of Powers' mission, over Turkish territory, are given. The hypothesis is put forward that, after reporting trouble with his oxygen supply, Powers lost consciousness and strayed across the Turkish-Soviet border. Planes are said to keep searching for the craft until the Soviets can identify the downed plane as the missing U-2.
METAPRAGMATIC DESCRIPTIONS:

(1) [U.S.: others/R/nM]
The United States *said* today an American weather-observation plane flown by a civilian apparently went astray near the Turkish-Soviet border Sunday when the pilot's oxygen supply failed.

(2) [U.S.S.R.: K/sQ/nM]
This was the official explanation of the incident *described* by Premier Khrushchev when he *said* an American "invader" had been shot down over the Soviet Union.

(3) [U.S.: others/R/nM]
The plane was flying at an altitude close to 55,000 feet, making weather observations over the Lake Van area of Turkey as part of a world-wide research program begun in 1956, a spokesman for the civilian space agency *said*.

(4) [U.S.: others/R/nM]
The spokesman *emphasized* that the plane was unarmed and carried no military equipment of any kind.

(5) [U.S.: others/R/nM]
He *said* it was marked with the letters N.A.S.A. in black on a goldyellow band and with an N.A.S.A. seal, a globe inside calipers.

(6) [U.S.S.R.: K/R/nM]
[Premier Khrushchev *said* the plane shot down bore no identification marks].

(7) [U.S.: others/R/nM]
The agency spokesman *denied* that the U-2 missing in Turkey carried any radioactivity-detection instruments.

(8) [U.S.: others/sQ/nM]
The *report made* today by the N.A.S.A. *said* that after the pilot had taken off from Incirlik Air Base, Turkey to study "gust-meteorological conditions" at a high altitude, he reported about 9 A.M. Sunday that he was having oxygen difficulties.

(9) [U.S.: others/R/nM]
The pilot *was said* to have reported on his emergency radio that he was headed for the Lake Van beacon [...].

(10) [U.S.: others/R/nM]
The report *noted* that there was no further word from the pilot.

(11) [U.S.: others/R/M:dM]
The Lake Van Area is mountainous and rugged, the agency *pointed out*, but although an aerial search was begun soon after receipt of the last communication, no sign of the aircraft was sighted.

(12) [U.S.: others/R/nM]
Not until Mr. Khrushchev's announcement today was there any suspicion that the Soviet Union was involved, Walter T. Bonney, the agency spokesman *said*.

(13) [U.S.: others/sQ/nM]
Even today, he *added*, planes were still searching for the craft in a possibly "wasted effort".

(14) [U.S.: others/Q/nM]
"If the Soviets would identify the U-2 as the plane they shot down, we would quit looking for it", Mr. Bonney *said*.

(15) [U.S.: others/sQ/M:dM]
The spokesman *observed* that if the pilot had continued to suffer a lack of oxygen the path of the plane from its last reported position would be "impossible to determine", but if it were on automatic pilot it would most likely have continued its northeasterly course.

(16) [U.S.: others/R/nM]
Mr. Bonney *explained* that N.A.S.A. had taken over the weather-observation program from its predecessor, the National Advisory Committee for Aeronautics.

(17) [U.S.: others/R/nM]
Mr. Bonney *said* considerable commercial traffic moved across Turkey in flights

between the Mediterranean and the Middle East.

(18) [U.S.: others/R/nM]
He *said* he was unaware, however, of the possibility that the pilot of the U-2 might have been lured across the Soviet border by false radio signals.

(19) [U.S.: E/R/nM]
President Eisenhower once *mentioned* at a news conference, in commenting on a previous plane incident, that the pilot might have been misled by a false radio signal.

(20) [U.S.: others/sQ/M:sM]
Lincoln White, State Department spokesman, *issued a brief statement* saying that the United States would take up the matter with the Soviet Union "with particular reference to the fate of the pilot".

(21) [U.S.: others/sQ/nM]
He *added* that the United States had "absolutely no information" on another alleged American violation of Soviet air space April 9 in the area of the Afghanistan-Soviet border.

COMMENTS:

As would be expected of newspaper reports (see section 3.2.), metapragmatic metaphors are conspicuous by their near-absence. One of them, *issued a brief statement* in (20), with its source domain in the realm of written documents, simply serves (since it is not clear whether the statement was actually in writing or not) to place the LAV focus on the official character of the message. In addition to this stock metaphor, there are two dead metaphors: *pointed out* in (11), with hand motion as its source domain; and *observed* in (15), which is basically a verb of perception (certainly more clearly than in the case of *noted* in (10), which is therefore treated as non-metaphorical). Both of these focus on the propositional content of A, and they strongly suggest the objective availability of a 'truth' which can simply be 'pointed at' (which is certainly the case in (11)) or which can easily be 'seen'. Thus they strengthen the impression of factuality created by the preponderance of neutral LAVs such as *said*, *explained*, *mentioned*, and the like.

This report is about the American explanation of the events. Twice Khrushchev's opinion is inserted in such a way as to cast doubt on his version of what happened. The semi-quote in (2) would not necessarily have indicated the reporter's doubts about the appropriateness of the category 'invader' (semi-quotes appear throughout the text), had it not immediately followed an unqualified presentation of the 'weather-observation plane' which 'apparently went astray'. Similarly, the bracketing of Khrushchev's contradiction of a NASA spokesman's statement, would — by itself — not necessarily have scored such an effect either. But in conjunction with a further suggestion of foul play on the part of the Soviets (officially denied in (18) but lent some respectability by referring to an earlier presidential statement in (19) — the only place where Eisenhower himself is quoted rather than some official spokesman) a rather clear picture emerges of a reporter who, to all appearances, attaches more credibility to the official U.S. version than to Khrushchev's account. This is emphasized once more by the use of 'alleged' in (21).

4.1.2. Article 2 (front page)

TITLE: see 4.1.1.
SUBTITLE: Premier is bitter
SUB-SUBTITLE: *Assails* 'provocation aimed at wrecking' May 16 parley.
[U.S.S.R.: K/sQ/M:dM]
AUTHOR: Osgood Caruthers
CONTENTS: Caruthers reports a speech made by Khrushchev before the opening session of the Supreme Soviet. Though it was originally planned as a speech on domestic policies, Khrushchev had widened the topic to international affairs, with special reference to the scheduled summit in Paris. He focused on indications that the U.S. was not serious about the summit, such as recent foreign policy statements, and Eisenhower's announcement that he would stay in Paris for only one week (letting Nixon take over in case the meeting would last longer). In this context he took his audience by surprise by announcing the shooting down of an American intruder into Soviet airspace.

METAPRAGMATIC DESCRIPTIONS:

(22) [U.S.S.R.: K/sQ/nM]
Premier Khrushchev *said* today that a United States plane on a mission of "aggressive provocation aimed at wrecking the summit conference" invaded Soviet territory May 1 and was shot down.

(23) [U.S.S.R.: K/R/M:sM]
The Premier, *in the most blistering speech against* American policies he *had made* since his meetings with President Eisenhower last autumn, *declared* that the incursion [...] cast gloom on the prospects for the success of the summit meeting in Paris eleven days hence.

(24) [U.S.S.R.: K/R/nM]
The *most sensational section of* Mr. Khrushchev's three-and-a-half-hour *speech* [...] was that concerning the *charges* of United States violations of Soviet airspace.

(25) [U.S.S.R.: K/R/nM]
The Premier *predicted* to foreign diplomats earlier this week that his talk on foreign

and domestic policies would contain major surprises.

(26) [U.S.S.R.: K/R/M:sM]
Indeed, *his report* of the plane incident *came as a shock* to Westerners and Soviet citizens alike.

(27) [U.S.: others/R/M:dM]
The United States Ambassador, Llewellyn E. Thompson Jr., *would make no comment* on the development.

(28) [U.S.S.R.: K/R/nM]
Mr. Krushchev *declared* that actually there had been two incidents involving intrusions by United States military planes during the last month.

(29) [U.S.S.R.: K/R/nM]
One plane, he *said*, flew from the direction of Afghanistan and was permitted to leave without military action or subsequent diplomatic protest.

(30) [U.S.S.R.: K/sQ/nM]
On May Day morning, he *said with emotion*, "when our people were celebrating their most beloved holiday", another plane crossed the southern borders and, on quickly delivered orders from the highest authority in Moscow, was shot down.

(31) [U.S.S.R.: K/R/M:dM]
The Premier *gave no details* as to the type of plane, which *was said* to bear no markings, or the fate of its crew.

(32) [U.S.: others/R/nM]
[The United States *said* the plane was a U-2 weather-observation plane carrying a crew of one.]

(33) [U.S.S.R.: K/sQ/nM]
He *declared* that it was presumed by the Kremlin that both planes had been based in either Turkey, Iran or Pakistan "which are linked with the United States in the aggressive" Central Treaty Organization.

(34) [U.S.S.R.: K/R/nM]
Mr. Khrushchev *said* the Soviet Union intended not only to protest to the United States over the second incident but also to take the matter before the United Nations Security Council.

(35) [U.S.S.R.: K/sQ/M:sM]
His Government also *will extend "serious warnings" to* countries that permit the American planes to be based on their territory, he *added*.

(36) [U.S.S.R.: K/sQ/M:sM]
These heated disclosures raised an explosive outcry of "bandits", "aggressors" and other angry expletives among the more than 1,300 deputies [...].

(37) [U.S.S.R.: K/Q/M:sM]
"Comrade Deputies," Mr. Khrushchev *declared, reading from a prepared speech, in an emotion-laden voice*, "the impression is being formed that the aggressive actions

newly taken by the United States against the Soviet Union are a foretaste of the summit meeting. [...]."

(38) [U.S.S.R.: K/sQ/M:dM]
The Premier *expressed gratitude* to the military unit that had fulfilled the task of "securing the borders of our country with honor" by shooting down the plane on May Day.

(39) [U.S.S.R.: K/R/nM]
This gave him the opportunity to *repeat a threat* that the Soviet Union would retaliate with its new rocket force against any attack and that foreign bases from which such an attack was launched would also be destroyed.

(40) [U.S.S.R.: K/sQ/nM]
Nevertheless, Mr. Khrushchev *urged* against an emotional reaction to his disclosures and *said* he still planned to go to the summit meeting "with a pure heart" [...].

(41) [U.S.S.R.: K/R/nM]
He *said* he did not consider the intrusion a reconnaissance in prelude to war.

(42) [U.S.S.R.: K/sQ/nM]
The Premier *added* that he believed the American people, "except for certain imperialist, monopolist circles", wanted peace and friendship with the Soviet Union.

COMMENTS:

When comparing this article (providing the Soviet point of view) with the previous one (focusing on an official American perspective), various differences in the reporters' metapragmatic choices are patent. First, only one source is quoted on the Soviet side, Premier Khrushchev himself, whereas the American head of state, President Eisenhower, hardly plays a part in the explanation of the events as reported in Article 1.

Second, the mode in which communicative content is presented is overwhelmingly reported speech in Article 1. In this article, however, there are about as many quotes and semi-quotes as simply reported messages. This contrast, though not very significant in itself, helps to strengthen a vague impression — already created in Article 1 — that the content of the American official statements can be plainly and factually described whereas there are good reasons for the reporters to distance themselves from Khrushchev's words by clearly marking them as *his own*.

A third difference provides the reason — and at least a partial justification — for this practice. Whereas the average LAV focus in Article 1 (even of the few metapragmatic metaphors used) was on the propositional content of A, Sa's (i.e. Khrushchev's) emotions and often also his corresponding linguistic choices at the level of style are now heavily emphasized: *in the most blistering speech* ... in (23); *said with emotion* in (30); *heated disclosures* in

(36); *declared ...in an emotion-laden voice* in (37); and *expressed gratitude* in (38).

Fourth, related to this emphasis on emotions is the higher frequency of metapragmatic metaphors.

Fifth, also related to the same emphasis is the attention paid to Ha's (i.e. Khrushchev's audience's) reactions to Sa's utterances (completely left out of the picture in Article 1, partly because an equally clear body of 'hearers' could not be identified for the American official statements): *his report ... came as a shock* in (26); *these heated disclosures raised an explosive outcry* in (36); also *sensational* in (24) seems to be audience-related.

Finally, in addition to the 'neutral' and factual comments made by American officials, an overt tone of hostility is suggested with reference to Khrushchev's speech. Thus the (dead) metaphor *assails* in the title has physical attack as its source domain and places the LAV focus on Sa's hostile attitude. Similarly, the placing of *serious warnings* in (35) between quotation marks indicates, in this case, the author's disagreement with the choice of words to describe what he interprets, as appears from (39), as a plain *threat*.

In its own right, there is — with respect to our topic of investigation — little in this report that can be criticized. It is probably true that Khrushchev spoke emotionally and that he vented unmistakable anger in his customary fashion. But in conjunction with the subtle insinuation of his lower credibility in Article 1, the story may induce the reader to believe that the content of Khrushchev's disclosure is a subjective interpretation partly derived from unfriendly feelings. Another dimension is added in Article 3.

4.1.3. *Article 3 (front page)*

TITLE: U.S. *asks details* of plane incident. [U.S.: others/R/nM]
SUBTITLE: Data sought from envoy in Moscow as Washington *reacts with restraint*. [U.S.: others/R/M:sM]
AUTHOR: William J. Jorden
CONTENTS: Description of Washington's reaction to Khrushchev's disclosures about the plane incident, in the light of his earlier speech (in Baku) on the Berlin question — one point on the agenda for the Paris summit. The article emphasizes the interpretation that both the Baku and Supreme Soviet speeches are political maneuvering in preparation for the summit: by taking a tough stand in advance, any concessions at the summit would have a greater impact. Pressure on Khrushchev from his colleagues is speculated about. The possible impact on Eisenhower's plans for his Moscow visit is hinted at.

METAPRAGMATIC DESCRIPTIONS:

(43) [U.S.: others/R/M:sM]
Washington *reacted with restraint* today to Premier Khrushchev's announcement that a United States plane had been shot down Sunday on Soviet territory.

(44) [U.S.: others/R/nM]
There were some angry words on Capitol Hill — including a suggestion that President Eisenhower refuse to go to the summit meeting with Mr. Khrushchev in Paris May 16.

(45) [U.S.: others/R/nM]
But the Administration *would say little more* than that additional information was being sought from Moscow.

(46) [U.S.: others/R/M:sM]
A *message went to* Ambassador Llewellyn E. Thompson Jr. in Moscow this afternoon instructing him to request more details from the Soviet authorities.

(47) [U.S.: others/R/M:sM]
Their [i.e. U.S. officials'] *first reaction was* that he [Khrushchev] seemed to be preparing the way for placing the blame for a summit failure on the Western powers.

(48) [U.S.S.R.: K/R/M:dM]
He also *seemed to be giving advance warning* that the Allied leaders could expect little softness from him at the Paris meeting.

(49) [U.S.: others/R/nM]
The *consensus was* that the Khrushchev address was the latest move in pre-summit maneuvering, [...].

(50) [U.S.S.R.: K/R/nM]
Mr. Khrushchev *said* that the Governments of the United States, Britain and France did not seem to be looking forward to settlement of major East-West differences at the summit.

(51) [U.S.: others/R/nM]
The State Department *admitted the possibility* that the plane, *identified here as* an unarmed U-2 weather reconnaissance craft of the National Aeronautics and Space Administration, might have crossed the Soviet frontier by accident.

(52) [U.S.: others/R/M:dM]
The question was raised, however, why the weaponless craft had been shot down and not merely forced to land.

(53) [U.S.: others/R/nM]
Diplomats also *questioned* the propriety of the Soviet Premier's decision to announce the incident publicly before informing the United States.

(54) [U.S.: others/R/M:dM]
The White House *declined any comment* on this problem [the influence of Khrushchev's stand on Berlin and the downing of the plane on Eisenhower's plans

for a trip to Moscow] this afternoon.

(55) [U.S.: others/R/nM]
James C. Hagarty, press secretary, *refused to say* anything about the downed aircraft or the President's plans.

(56) [U.S.: others/R/nM]
It remains to be seen, officials here *said*, how much of the Baku and Supreme Soviet speeches are firm policy and how much was designed to lay the groundwork for the summit meeting.

(57) [U.S.: others/R/nM]
Senator Styles Bridges, Republican of New Hampshire, *said* he thought President Eisenhower should refuse to go to the Paris meeting until he had a proper explanation of the Soviet action.

(58) [U.S.: others/sQ/nM]
Senator Mike Mansfield, Democrat of Montana, *said* prospects for the summit were poor indeed "if the Russians are going to shoot first and complain later".

(59) [U.S.: others/R/nM]
Senator Mansfield also *said* the plane incident raised the question of adequate controls over such flights.

(60) [U.S.: others/R/nM]
He *said* reports indicated that President Eisenhower had not been aware of the flight.

(61) [U.S.: others/Q/nM]
"Can any agency of this Government, without the knowledge of politically responsible officials, assume for itself the right to probe for scientific or whatever purposes along a dangerous border and, hence, endanger the policies of the President?" Senator Mansfield *asked*.

(62) [U.S.: others/sQ/nM]
Senator E.L. Bartlett, Democrat of Alaska, *said* he thought the United States should proceed with the summit meeting despite "the crude, rude, provocative remarks of Khrushchev."

COMMENTS:

Serious asking presupposes ignorance of the answer. Thus the report that the U.S. *asks details* (see title) of the plane incident and that the *message* that *went to* Ambassador Thompson (in (46)) instructs him to request details from the Soviet authorities, corroborates the picture of an innocent U.S. government which does not have a clue as to what really happened beyond the facts of Powers' mission and his oxygen trouble as revealed in the NASA statement.

Most of what has been said about the contrast between Articles 1 and 2 could be repeated with reference to 2 and 3. Thus, for instance, the proportion of semi-quotes in 3 is much lower than in 2. And one of the semi-quotes used, citing Senator Bartlett's description of Khrushchev's remarks as *crude, rude, provocative* (see (62)), seems to be inserted for reasons of agreement rather than disagreement (though the semi-quotational distancing device is needed because the word choice might have been judged inappropriate for the style of international news reporting). Indeed, only the reporter's agreement with the underlying message of hostility (hinging on the use of *provocative*, a dead metaphor with its source domain in the area of fights and conflicts) and bad manners (as revealed by the use of *crude*, basically indicating roughness of material but metaphorically extended to aspects of communicative style), can explain the implications of *reacts with restraint* (subtitle) and *reacted with restraint* in (43). These metapragmatic stock metaphors, grounded in a primary source domain of acting in response or in opposition to some former act, and in a secondary source domain of emotional response, place the LAV focus on the contextual link with Khrushchev's declarations of which it is suggested that they provided good reasons for an emotional, unrestrained reaction. That the emotions were there is indicated by *there were some angry words* in (44). But their voicing is said to be restrained in spite of the 'good reasons' to be found in Khrushchev's hostility, already hinted at by the choice of certain metapragmatic descriptions in Article 2 and further elaborated by identifying his motives as political maneuvering in (47), (48), (49) and (56) and by depicting the downing of the plane as an unwarranted act of aggression in (52) and (58), and in the Soviet Premier's bad manners as presented in (53). It should be emphasized that, in this article, suggestions of hostility and bad manners are always embedded in metapragmatic descriptions, thus shielding the reporter from a simple identification of his own interpretations with the ones reported. But the LAVs chosen to govern those descriptions focus on the propositional content, thus emphasizing its factual basis. At any rate, no attempt is made to put it in a different interpretive perspective.

4.1.4. *Article 4*

TITLE: U.S. *says* plane downed by Soviet was weather craft on research mission. [U.S.: others/R/nM]
SUBTITLE: U-2 is civilian-piloted, unarmed research jet plane.
AUTHOR: Unsigned report
CONTENTS: Details about the U-2: an unarmed, civilian-piloted, high-altitude research plane powered by a single turbojet engine and flown by one man, first built by Lockheed in 1954; can cruise above 50,000 feet but its top

speed is less than the speed of light; ordered by the Air Force for weather observation; used by NASA since 1956 for investigating the turbulence of the jet stream, cloud density, radio-active fall-out, cosmic rays; despite its non-military status, much about it is classified as secret; used for research in the U.S. and abroad; five U-2 accidents have been reported.

COMMENTS:

Except for the title, no metapragmatic descriptions are used at all. In other words, all information (with which, moreover, no individual reporter's name is associated) is presented as factual and objective. And since the facts presented are entirely in line with the official explanation of the events, this article underscores the tendency to attach more credibility to the American version than to Khrushchev's accusation.

4.1.5. *Article 5*

TITLE: U.N. Council will get Soviet complaint today.
AUTHOR: Unsigned
CONTENTS: Only the following sentences, and a brief note about an earlier Soviet complaint to the Security Council (in 1955) concerning U.S. aircraft flying in the direction of Soviet borders.

METAPRAGMATIC DESCRIPTIONS:

(63) [U.S.S.R.: others/R/nM]
A Soviet spokesman *indicated* tonight that a complaint regarding alleged violation of Soviet airspace by a United States plane would be submitted to the Security Council tomorrow.

(64) [?/R/M:dM]
Some sources *expressed the belief* that the Soviet Union would merely address a letter to the Security Council, and would not ask for a meeting.

(65) [U.S.S.R.: others/R/nM]
The Soviet spokesman *commented*, however, that Premier Khrushchev had said that the Soviet Union would ask the Council to take measures regarding the plane.

COMMENTS:

This is the first report in which, on the Soviet side, not Khrushchev himself is cited. Whether the absence of emotion-centered LAVs is explicable in terms of that fact, cannot be determined because the text of Article 5 is too concise.

Somewhat puzzling is the insertion of (64). It is impossible to decide whether the sources mentioned are Soviet or American — though probably American. And what purpose does the informational content serve? It only raises expectations about one possible answer to a question the real answer to which would be readily available one day later. Why not wait that one more day instead of promoting a semi-prediction? Probably this is an example where reporting is guided by the reporter's hopes, in this case the hope that a major crisis in international relations could be averted. But such a hope could only be based on a belief (again hinted at by the use of 'alleged' in (63)) in the sincerity of the U.S. explanation of the event.

4.1.6. *Further comments*

A few remarks are needed on other materials related to the U-2 incident in this issue of the *New York Times*. In addition to the five reports presented, it also contains:
(i) "Excerpts on foreign topics from Khrushchev's speech to the Supreme Soviet".
(ii) "Khrushchev's remarks on U.S. plane" (also excerpted from his speech).
(iii) "Text of the U.S. statement on plane." To this text, a map of the flight route is added with the following lines underneath: "The Soviet Union said it had shot down a United States aircraft that had intruded into its territory (cross) [this cross is placed just across the Turkish-Soviet border]. The broken line and arrows indicate the planned route of a missing United States weather plane." This map certainly contributes to the impression of factuality created in connection with the NASA statement.
(iv) "List of clashes on planes given", subtitled "U.S.-Soviet incidents began with loss of navy plane over Baltic in 1950."
(v) "British discount Khrushchev talk", subtitled "Officials are said to believe speech was only typical pre-summit maneuver." This article on the British reaction re-emphasizes motives of political maneuvering and 'Mr. Khrushchev's offensiveness and boasting'. It enlists British support for disbelieving Khrushchev's version by talking once more about an 'alleged intrusion'. The only new element is the view that if the flight had been 'deliberate' it was 'an act of folly'.
(vi) "Paris sees cloudy outlook."
Briefly, the general picture which emerged from the articles discussed is certainly not changed by these additional materials.

4.2. May 7th

4.2.1. *Article 6 (front page)*

TITLE: President hints visit to Moscow is not certainty.

SUBTITLE: 'If I go', he says
SUB-SUBTITLE: But officials doubt he will cancel trip over plane incident
AUTHOR: William J. Jorden
CONTENTS: President Eisenhower is reported to have mentioned his intention to give Khrushchev a boat as a present, if he would go to Moscow. The White House has not clarified the hint about the possibility of his not going. Officials are quoted as expressing doubts as to whether the plane incident would really have any effect, but adding that Khrushchev's attitude in Paris would be crucial. The expectation is formulated that the Soviet Premier would be less 'threatening' and 'belligerent' at the summit than in his address to the Supreme Soviet. State Department spokesmen are said to keep contradicting the Soviet version of the U-2 incident, which is again presented as a propaganda move and a pre-summit maneuver. The United States is said to have been maneuvering for wide support on the Paris issues as well. The Soviet and U.S. stands on Berlin are repeated.

METAPRAGMATIC DESCRIPTIONS:

(66) [U.S.: others/R/nM]
Other officials *said* they doubted that the President would cancel his visit as a result of the downing of a United States plane reportedly by a Soviet rocket May 1.

(67) [U.S.S.R.: others/sQ/nM]
Moscow *said* the plane had intruded into Soviet airspace on an "aggressive" mission designed to disrupt the atmosphere for the summit talks.

(68) [U.S.: others/R/M:sM]
The Government *continued to be reserved and noncommittal* on the plane incident.

(69) [U.S.: others/R/nM]
A note *asking for* additional details on the plane and the fate of the pilot was delivered to the Soviet Foreign Ministry today.

(70) [U.S.: others/R/nM]
A State Department spokesman *did dispute* Soviet allegations that the plane was on an aggressive, provocative mission.

(71) [U.S.: others/R/nM]
The spokesman, Lincoln White, *said* it was assumed here that the civilian pilot had lost consciousness as a result of a failure in his oxygen equipment.

(72) [U.S.: others/R/nM]
"There was no deliberate attempt to violate Soviet air space," Mr. White *said*, "and there never has been".

COMMENTS:
This article adds little to the picture of the events emerging from the

reports in *The New York Times* on May 6th. Again reported speech governed by non-metaphorical LAVs predominates in the description of the American position, whereas a semi-quote (for "an 'aggressive' mission" in (67)) is judged necessary for the one reference to the Soviet version. Furthermore, the stock metaphor *be reserved and noncommittal* in (68), literally describing Sa's disposition but extended to an account of communicative behavior indicative of that disposition, focuses on the restraint exercised by the U.S. government in the face of Khrushchev's hostility and bad manners (explicitly referred to as "a truculent or threatening attitude" and as "threatening or belligerent"). And the government's ignorance of what happened after Powers reported oxygen trouble is implicitly re-emphasized by their *asking for* (see (69)) details.

4.2.2. *Article 7 (front page)*

TITLE: Foreign-based U-2's grounded for study.
AUTHOR: Jack Raymond
CONTENTS: All foreign-based U-2 weather observation planes are said to have been grounded for checking the oxygen supply system. Some details of NASA's story are repeated. There is said to be a discrepancy in time between the events as told by Khrushchev and by U.S. officials. An explanation referring to another U-2 flight on the same day is rejected. Pentagon sources are cited saying that downing a U-2 would not require any special rocketry skill: though it can fly at high altitudes, the plane is clumsy and slow. Results of research carried out with the U-2's are described. At the end, the topic is shifted to the Air Force's reconnaissance operations near the borders, which are said to be no more provocative than Soviet espionage practices.

METAPRAGMATIC DESCRIPTIONS:

(73) [U.S.: others/R/nM]
A spokesman for the National Aeronautics and Space Administration *said* the weather research flights abroad were halted to permit checking of equipment, particularly the oxygen system.

(74) [U.S.: others/R/nM]
The spokesman *called attention to* earlier announcements that the U-2 high-altitude weather-observation plane missing in the Turkish-Soviet border area was believed to have had a faulty oxygen line that may have caused the pilot to black out.

(75) [U.S.: others/R/nM]
This is the plane, a single-engine turbojet piloted by a civilian employe of the Lockheed Aircraft Corporation under contract to the N.A.S.A., that United States officials *said* might have strayed over the Soviet border and been downed as an "invader".

DATA AND COMMENTS 59

(76) [U.S.: others/R/nM]
An N.A.S.A. spokesman *said* that the equipment of the plane at Edwards Air Base had been checked.

(77) [U.S.: others/R/nM]
The spokesman *denied* that the grounding of the foreign-based U-2's, which are designed to fly at altitudes of 55,000 feet, had anything to do with Moscow's sensitivity to flights near the borders of the Soviet Union.

(78) [U.S.: others/R/nM]
The United States Air Force, at the same time, *emphatically denied* that its operations, including varieties of reconnaissance and patrols, were being reduced anywhere on the Soviet periphery because of Soviet protests or to prevent any possible new incidents in view of the pending summit meeting.

(79) [U.S.: others/R/nM]
Officials here *were unable to clarify* the discrepancy in the time given by Premier Khrushchev yesterday for the radar sighting of the plane he said had been trespassing at the Soviet-Turkish border and the time when the missing U-2 was reported to be in the air.

(80) [U.S.S.R.: K/R/nM]
Mr. Khrushchev *told* the Supreme Soviet that at 0536 hours Moscow time, May 1, an American plane flew over the frontier.

(81) [U.S.S.R.: others/R/nM]
Marshal Andrei A. Grechko *added* today that the United States plane was sighted by radar as soon as it crossed the frontier at an altitude of about five miles.

(82) [U.S.: others/R/nM]
United States Air Force officials at the Pentagon *said* that they knew of no Air Force flights in the Turkish area at the time and that no Air Force planes were missing.

(83) [U.S.S.R.: others/sQ/nM]
Marshal Grechko *told* the Supreme Soviet that Soviet rocket troops had brought the "invader" plane down with one shot after Premier Khrushchev personally gave the order to shoot.

(84) [U.S.: others/R/nM]
In the first place, military observers here *noted*, the Russians at the border would hardly have gone to the trouble to check with Moscow if they thought the lone plane actually were an "invader".

(85) [U.S.: others/R/nM]
Thus observers here *said*, it appeared that the action announced by Mr. Khrushchev was political and not military.

(86) [U.S.: others/R/nM]
Secondly, Pentagon sources *said*, the U-2 — if indeed that was the plane the Russians say they downed — would have afforded an easy mark for ground-to-air weapons.

(87) [U.S.: others/R/nM]
It has been reported that the plane can actually rise to close to 100,000 feet.

(88) [U.S.: others/R/nM]
Aware of considerable speculation about the weather observation program, for which the U-2 high altitude planes have been used, N.A.S.A. *called attention to* some of the scientific conclusions reached thus far.

(89) [U.S.: others/R/nM]
The program was begun in 1956, the space agency *noted*.

(90) [U.S.: others/sQ/nM]
At the same time, passengers in such aircraft would be "discommoded," the agency's spokesman *said*.

(91) [U.S.: others/sQ/nM]
A space agency spokesman *said* that the Turkish site was used for the studies because a world-wide sampling of air weather conditions was being sought and one "obviously can't pick sites in Russia".

(92) [U.S.: others/sQ/nM]
He *said* that the research flights in Turkey began late in 1957 and would "continue indefinitely until we run out of new information".

(93) [U.S.: others/sQ/nM]
Reacting to speculation about the Air Force's reconnaissance operations near the Soviet borders, Pentagon sources *suggested* there was no reason to be "defensive" about the United States efforts.

(94) [U.S.: others/R/nM]
These sources *emphasized* that the Soviet Union has persistently hidden its activities.

(95) [U.S.: others/sQ/nM]
At the same time, Pentagon officials *called attention to* the Soviet Union's own efforts at "passive espionage" on United States operations.

(96) [U.S.: others/R/nM]
They *cited* the recent trawler incident, in which a heavily instrumented Soviet ship passed close by missile-launched tests of the United States' first Polaris submarine off Long Island.

In addition to these, there is the following line accompanying a photograph of a wrecked plane:

(97) [U.S.S.R.: others/R/nM]
This photograph printed in the Moscow newspaper Trud, *is described as* showing the wreckage of a United States airplane shot down on Sunday over Soviet territory.

COMMENTS:

Virtually every sentence in this article is embedded under a metapragmatically descriptive verb or phrase, thus transforming the incident into an indisputably communicative event. Inserting *said*, *called attention to*, *denied*, etc. on every possible occasion might create the impression that the author wants to dissociate himself from the content of the reported opinions. Though such a conclusion could be valid, whether the average reader of *The New York Times* would get that impression, would not only depend on properties of this article but on those in combination or in contrast with characteristics of related reports in the same issue. For that reason, Article 7 will be briefly commented upon in comparison with Article 8 which focuses on the Soviet side of the conflict.

4.2.3. Article 8 (front page)

TITLE: Rocket downed jet, Soviet *says*. [U.S.S.R.: others/R/nM]
SUBTITLE: It *reports* that Khrushchev ordered attack — Public *is urged* to express 'wrath'. [U.S.S.R.: others/R/nM] + [U.S.S.R.: others/sQ/nM]
AUTHOR: Max Frankel
CONTENTS: Further comments, drawn from speeches to the Supreme Soviet, on the downing of an American plane over Soviet territory, are reported. The American embassy is said to be making inquiries for details. Soviet newspaper comments are cited. Special attention is paid to the way in which the plane was brought down: by means of a single ground-to-air rocket. Further details are said not to have been divulged to the Soviet people.

METAPRAGMATIC DESCRIPTIONS:

(98) [U.S.S.R.: others/sQ/M:dM]
With the summit meeting less than a fortnight away, Moscow *encouraged* the Soviet people today to express their "wrath" over the incident in which it was charged that Soviet territory was violated by an unarmed United States plane May 1.

(99) [U.S.S.R.: others/R/nM]
At the same time it *said* that the intruding plane had been brought down by a single rocket shot fired on the order of Premier Khrushchev.

(100) [U.S.S.R.: others/sQ/nM]
"We have enough rockets for every plane" that flies into Soviet airspace "and we are going to use them against the enemies," *declared* Marshal Andrei A. Grechko, commander of Soviet ground forces.

(101) [U.S.S.R.: others/Q/nM]
"If the Western powers think we are weak because we show patience", *said* Foreign Minister Andrei A. Gromyko, "they are miscalculating".

(102) [U.S.S.R.: others/sQ/nM]
From the rostrum of the Great Kremlin Palace, leading Soviet officials *repeatedly told* the Supreme Soviet, the country's version of a Parliament, that the German invasion of 1941 also had been preceded by "provocations" from the air.

(103) [U.S.: others/R/nM]
In the [American] embassy and in other Western missions here, diplomats *made no secret of* their serious concern over the sudden pre-summit drop in temperature.

(104) [U.S.: others/R/nM]
The United States Embassy *sent a note* to the Foreign Ministry this morning *inquiring* whether the downed plane was a single-engine U-2 jet weather plane [...].

(105) [U.S.: others/R/nM]
The note also *inquired about* the plane's pilot, Francis G. Powers, a civilian employe of the Lockheed Aircraft Corporation.

(106) [U.S.S.R.: K/R/M:sM]
Premier Khrushchev *set the public tone* for his Government yesterday *in a bitter speech* to the Supreme Soviet.

(107) [U.S.S.R.: K/sQ/nM]
He *said* American planes made "hostile" flights into Soviet airspace on April 9 and May 1.

(108) [U.S.S.R.: K/R/nM]
He *called* the flights acts of aggression and deliberate attempts to sabotage the relaxed international atmosphere.

(109) [U.S.S.R.: K/R/nM]
Tolerance for the first intrusion served only to encourage "the aggressor", he *said*, and therefore the Government ordered the May Day intruder shot down.

(110) [U.S.S.R.: others/R/M:sM]
More deliberate but still angry comment about the incident *was given* today by most of the seventeen speakers who followed him to the rostrum.

(111) [U.S.S.R.: others/R/nM]
The trade union newspaper Trud printed a photograph of a mound of tangled wreckage this morning and *told* its readers that it was the remains of the plane found by civilian searching parties.

(112) [U.S.S.R.: others/R/nM]
Other newspapers had photographs of and articles about artillery soldiers who *were credited with* having shot the plane down.

(113) [U.S.S.R.: others/R/nM]
They *were praised* for hitting a target moving at 900 kilometers (562 miles) an hour at a "very high altitude".

(114) [U.S.S.R.: others/R/M:dM]
No one here *has disclosed* the plane's flight path over Soviet soil.

(115) [U.S.S.R.: others/sQ/nM]
The public *has not been told* whether the plane was armed, how it was adjudged to be "hostile," at what point it crossed the Soviet frontier and where it crashed.

(116) [U.S.S.R.: others/R/M:dM]
Mr. Gromyko *dismissed as nonsense* an early Washington report that the plane's pilot might have been unconscious because he had run out of oxygen an hour after his take-off in Turkey.

(117) [U.S.S.R.: others/sQ/nM]
Marshal Grechko, the only military man among the speakers, *described* the May Day incident as an act of "enemy intelligence" and "cold war".

(118) [U.S.S.R.: K/sQ/nM]
In general, however, where Premier Khrushchev *had used the word* "aggression", the speakers *used the word* "provocation".

(119) [U.S.S.R.: others/R/nM]
Marshal Grechko *said* the order to bring down the plane had come from Mr. Khrushchev himself.

(120) [U.S.S.R.: others/R/nM]
The first rocket shot, presumably of a ground-to-air rocket, fulfilled the command, he *related*.

COMMENTS:

Article 8 shows a much wider variety of metapragmatic description types than Article 7. The repertoire in Article 7 was restricted to reported speech governed by non-metaphorical LAVs and some semi-quotes also headed by non-metaphorical LAVs. Without a single exception, all those LAVs focused on the propositional content of the message. And with the exception of *were unable to clarify* in (79), the factual basis of American statements is never called into doubt by the use of clear distancing devices. In contrast, the Soviet categorization of the plane as an 'invader' in (83) immediately calls for a semi-quote. Also in the reporting of American claims semi-quotes are used (see (90), (91), (92), (93), and (95)), but none of these deals directly with the U-2 in question.

Though reported speech and semi-quotes embedded under non-metaphorical LAVs also prevail in Article 8, the informational pattern is markedly different. Most LAVs also focus on propositional content. But whereas U.S. denials are reported as *denied* in (77) and *emphatically denied* in (78) (Article 7), a denial by Gromyko in Article 8 is described in (117) as *dismissed as nonsense*, a dead metaphor which can still be viewed as content-oriented but which also carries the attitudinal implication of unwillingness to seriously consider what is rejected. Elsewhere, emotions are foregrounded: *more deliberate but still angry comment ... was given* in (110); and Khrushchev is said to have *set the public tone ... in a bitter speech* in (106). What is new in this article is the framing of the emotion-oriented descriptions. Emotional utterances are presented as demagogical devices. Not only does the reporter explicitly mention that *Moscow encouraged the Soviet people today to express their "wrath"* in (98). But *set the public tone* in (106) presents the same information more implicitly. And so does *deliberate* in (110), suggesting that the expression of anger is merely calculated rather than spontaneous. In this way Article 8 provides the foundations for the credibility of the opinion reported in Article 7 that "it appeared that the action announced by Mr. Khrushchev [the shooting of the plane] was political and not military" (in (85)). Though the author of Article 7 may have intended to distance himself from the opinion by clearly attributing it to others (though those 'others' are not named), the communicative effect of the two articles together is likely to be the impression of factual truth. Similarly, Article 8 corroborates speculations (presented in the May 6 issue and repeated in Article 6) about Khrushchev's speech as a typical pre-summit maneuver.

In contrast to the semi-quotes in Article 7, those in Article 8 deal directly with the missing plane and most of them serve as distancing devices dissociating the author from the categories and attributes used by the cited Soviet sources: *provocation(s)* in (102) and (118), *aggressor* in (109), *aggression* in (118), *hostile* in (107) and (115), and *enemy intelligence* and *cold war* in (117).

Adding to the impression that there is something fishy about the Soviet declarations, the author points at the lack of details in them (in (114) and (115)).

4.2.4. *Further comments*

In addition to those reports, the May 7 issue of *The New York Times* included only one related document, the "Text of the U.S. note" which was delivered to the Soviet Foreign Ministry, asking for more details to identify the downed plane as the missing U-2, and for information concerning the fate of the pilot.

Summarizing the reporting on May 6 and May 7 we can say that Hd (the readership of *The New York Times*) is offered a coherent picture by various Sd's (reporters of *The New York Times*, usually identified by name) of a communicative conflict between two groups of Sa's (American and Soviet officials), each trying to convince Ha (the international community, including Hd, the readership of *The New York Times*) of the truth of a particular version of a real-world event. Presumably, the American Sa's also try to convince the Soviets of the truth of their version in response to a Soviet accusation. The way in which the different Sd's frame the communicative interaction, by the choice of metapragmatic terms in combination with modes of content presentation, shows their inclination to attach more credibility to the American story than to the Soviet claims. The average Hd can be expected to come to share this inclination.

4.3. May 8th

4.3.1. *Article 9 (front page)*

TITLE: U.S. *concedes* flight over Soviet, *defends* search for intelligence; Russians hold downed pilot as spy. [U.S.: others/R/nM] + [U.S.: others/R/M:dM] (Note: this title covers both Article 9 and Article 10, presenting Soviet and U.S. messages, respectively, and written by two different reporters.)
SUBTITLE: 'Confession' *cited*. [U.S.S.R.: others/sQ/nM]
SUB-SUBTITLE: Khrushchev *charges* jet was 1,200 miles from the border. [U.S.S.R.: K/R/M:dM]
AUTHOR: Osgood Caruthers
CONTENTS: Report of additional revelations by Khrushchev saying that the U-2 was shot down 1,200 miles inside Soviet territory, that incriminating reconnaissance equipment was found in the wreckage, and that the pilot, who was captured alive, confessed to have been on a spying mission. Details of the confession are given. Some reactions of Soviet citizens are discribed.

METAPRAGMATIC DESCRIPTIONS:

The article is accompanied by a picture with the following line:

(121) [U.S.S.R.: K/R/nM]
Accuses pilot: Premier Khrushchev displaying before the Supreme Soviet in Moscow one of the views of Soviet territory he *said* had been obtained by United States flier.

From the text:

(122) [U.S.S.R.: K/R/nM]
Premier Khrushchev *jubilantly reported* today the capture of the pilot of a United States plane that he *said* had been shot down on May Day.

(123) [U.S.S.R.: K/R/nM]
He *said* the American had admitted attempting to carry out a photo-reconnaissance mission all the way across the Soviet Union from Pakistan to Norway.

(124) [U.S.S.R.: K/R/nM]
Mr. Khrushchev *said* the American was being held and probably would be tried, presumably for espionage, in Moscow.

(125) [U.S.S.R.: K/R/nM]
The Premier *said* the plane had been shot down by a Soviet rocket near Sverdlovsk, 1,200 miles from the Afghan-Soviet border.

(126) [U.S.S.R.: K/Q/nM]
To wildly cheering Deputies of the Supreme Soviet, who had been called into a three-day session to pass on internal legislation, Mr. Khrushchev *cried* : "We have parts of the plane and we also have the pilot, who is quite alive and kicking. The Pilot is in Moscow and so are the parts of the plane".

(127) [U.S.S.R.: K/R/nM]
He *implied* once again that he felt that the United States military had sent the plane across the Soviet Union as a provocation aimed at sabotaging the summit conference, which is scheduled to open a week from Monday in Paris.

(128) [U.S.S.R.: K/R/nM]
But he *indicated* that he still intended to meet with the Western leaders and play host to President Eisenhower.

(129) [U.S.S.R.: K/sQ/nM]
Mr. Khrushchev *said*, however, that the incident was "bad preparation" for the East-West talks.

(130) [U.S.S.R.: K/sQ/nM]
He displayed a handful of large photographs of what he *said* was part of the "espionage equipment" taken from the plane's wreckage and from the pilot.

(131) [U.S.S.R.: K/R/nM]
The Soviet leader *said* the plane had taken a cluster of photographs of industrial centers and airfields, missile bases and other installations and had made tape recordings of Soviet radio and radar stations.

(132) [U.S.S.R.: K/R/nM]
The pilot has told his captors, Mr. Khrushchev *added*, that he started from Pakistan on a mission that was to have taken him at extremely high altitudes across the Soviet Union to Archangel and Murmansk and on beyond the Arctic Circle to a base in Norway.

(133) [U.S.S.R.: K/R/M:sM]
Mr. Khrushchev *made his account a story of high drama and low skullduggery interspersed with bitingly sarcastic remarks* about Washington's contention that the pilot was on a regular weather reconnaissance mission and had probably gotten lost during a blackout due to the failure of his oxygen equipment.

(134) [U.S.S.R.: K/R/nM]
Mr. Khrushchev *said* the pilot had denied ever having felt dizziness from the lack of oxygen.

(135) [U.S.: others/R/nM]
Ambassador L.E. Thompson Jr. *said* the matter was for Washington to comment upon.

(136)   [U.S.S.R.: others/sQ/M:sM]
Cries of "shame, shame" *rose from* the tense deputies in the Grand Kremlin Palace as Premier Khrushchev produced a photograph of a small hypodermic needle he *said* Mr. Powers had carried to inject himself with poison in case of capture.

(137)   [U.S.S.R.: others/sQ/M:sM]
Cries of "bandits, bandits" *filled the huge hall* at the sight of a big photograph of what Mr. Khrushchev *called* a noiseless pistol for use against captors or on the pilot himself.

(138)   [U.S.S.R.: others/R/M:sM]
Cheers and applause greeted the Premier's *remark that* the photographic equipment taken from the plane and the pictures that had been taken were not bad, but Soviet ones were better.

(139)   [U.S.S.R.: K/R/M:sM]
He *had high praise* for the crew of the Sverdlovsk rocket base [...].

(140)   [U.S.S.R.: K/R/nM]
Crewmen and officers have been decorated for carrying out their duties, Mr. Khrushchev *said*.

(141)   [U.S.S.R.: K/R/nM]
Moreover, he *declared*, rockets are now a major arm in the Soviet forces and have been placed under the separate command of Marshal Mitrofan I. Nedelin.

(142)   [U.S.S.R.: K/R/nM]
The force will be strengthened despite a reduction in regular armed forces, he *added*.

(143)   [U.S.S.R.: K/sQ/M:sM]
Mr. Khrushchev *seized this opportunity also to repeat* that perhaps President Eisenhower had known nothing about this mission and that it had been the independent work of "madmen in the Pentagon".

(144)   [U.S.S.R.: K/R/nM]
The Soviet leader *said* he had not brought out all the details when he first reported at the opening of the Supreme Soviet two days ago that the American plane, said to be a Lockheed U-2 high altitude weather reconnaissance craft, had been shot down inside the Soviet border.

(145)   [U.S.S.R.: K/Q/nM]
"Comrades, I must tell you a secret," he *said*. "When I was making my report I deliberately did not say that the pilot was alive and in good health and that we have got parts of the plane. We did so deliberately because had we told everything at once, the Americans would have invented another version."

(146)   [U.S.S.R.: K/sQ/nM]
The pilot *was said* by Mr. Khrushchev also to have carried with him celophane wrapped packets of gold French franc coins ("done in a cultured American way"), 7,500 rubles and other foreign currencies and two extra gold wrist watches and several gold rings.

(147) [U.S.S.R.: K/Q/nM]
"Why was all this necessary in the upper layers of the atmosphere?" the Premier *asked derisively*. "Or maybe, the pilot was to have flown still higher to Mars and was going to lead astray Martian ladies?"

(148) [U.S.S.R.: K/R/nM]
Mr. Khrushchev *read off what he said was* the pilot's testimony to his captors to the effect that he was employed by the Central Intelligence Agency to work for military intelligence under the guise of a civilian pilot [...].

(149) [U.S.S.R.: K/R/nM]
In reality, *according to the testimony read* by the Soviet Premier, Mr. Powers was a member of the 10-10 unit based at Incirlik, east of Adana, Turkey.

(150) [U.S.S.R.: K/R/nM]
His commander *was identified as* Col. William Shelton [...].

(151) [U.S.S.R.: K/R/nM]
The pilot *was said* to have testified he had made numerous probes inside the Soviet Union [...].

(152) [U.S.S.R.: K/Q/M:dM]
Mr. Khrushchev *gave these additional details* of testimony he said had been extracted from Mr. Powers: "[...]".

(153) [U.S.S.R.: K/sQ/M:dM]
This gave rise to *a charge* by Mr. Khrushchev *that* Turkey, Pakistan and Norway, all military allies of the United States, were "participants in this hostile act."

COMMENTS:

The reported speech mode, combined with non-metaphorical LAVs, is used to present the content of the overwhelming majority of Khrushchev's utterances. Moreover, semi-quotes are used sparingly. And of those used, only 'confession' in the subtitle, 'espionage equipment' in (130), 'madmen in the Pentagon' in (143), and 'participants in this hostile act' in (153), could serve a distancing function comparable to that discussed in connection with earlier articles. In general, then, the distribution of metapragmatic description types comes a little closer to that observed in articles dealing with the American account of the event. The factual truth of Khrushchev's claims is no longer made to appear doubtful. Moreover, overt indications of hostility or bad manners have vanished from the scene.

However, the choice of metapragmatic descriptions (metaphorical and otherwise) takes a different turn: Khrushchev's style of delivery becomes a major LAV focus. Not only is Khrushchev reported to have *cried* (in (126)) that the pilot had been captured and parts of the plane recovered. He also *jubilantly reported* the capture (in (122)), *asked derisively* (in (147)) whether the pilot really needed all the money and valuables found on him in the upper layers of the atmosphere, and made other *bitingly sarcastic remarks* (in (133)). Also the reports of the audience's verbal reactions (in (136) to (138)) highlight matters of style.

As such, there is nothing wrong with these descriptions. They are probably quite accurate: the tone of Khrushchev's new disclosures was indeed sarcastic, almost from the beginning to the end, and there must have been triumph in his voice when announcing that the U.S. had been caught red-handed and when he felt he could expose all previous official explanation as lies. But the reader's attention is diverted (consciously or not) from the possibility of elaborate fabrications on the part of the U.S. government. There is not a single explicit reference to clearly intentional untruthfulness in the American version of the previous days. Instead, in (133) Khrushchev is said to have *made his account a story of high drama and low skullduggery interspersed with bitingly sarcastic remarks*. This description, loaded with metaphors, does not only identify the sarcasm in his style, but adds the suggestion of wild exaggerations as to the importance of the event ('high drama') and of overindulgence in his emphasis on U.S. deceptiveness ('low skullduggery'). Since exaggerations are deviations from the truth, Soviet manipulation is brought to the fore rather than the possibility of American duplicity.

4.3.2. *Article 10 (front page)*

TITLE: see 4.3.1.
SUBTITLE: Action *explained*. [U.S.: others/R/nM]
SUB-SUBTITLE: Officials *say* danger of surprise attack forces watch. [U.S.: others/R/nM]
AUTHOR: James Reston
CONTENTS: Summary of a State Department statement in response to Khrushchev's new disclosures, saying that a plane equipped for intelligence purposes was probably sent into Soviet airspace, but stressing that this had happened without authorization in Washington. President Eisenhower is said to have cleared the official declaration, in which also a justification is given for intelligence activities aimed at preventing a surprise attack. Such activities are said to be routine along the Soviet border, and the Soviets are said to be doing similar things. The background to the new U.S. statement is briefly described. And further speculations are reported on the ultimate impact of

the incident on the Paris summit.

METAPRAGMATIC DESCRIPTIONS:

(154) [U.S.: others/sQ/M:dM]
The United States *admitted* tonight that one of this country's planes equipped for intelligence purposes had "probably" flown over Soviet territory.

(155) [U.S.: others/sQ/nM]
An official statement *stressed*, however, that "there was no authorization for any such flight" from authorities in Washington.

(156) [U.S.: others/R/nM]
As to who might have authorized the flight, officials refused to comment.

(157) [U.S.: others/Q/nM]
"It appears", *said* the statement, "that in endeavoring to obtain information now concealed behind the Iron Curtain, a flight over Soviet territory was probably undertaken by an unarmed civilian U-2 plane".

(158) [U.S.: others/R/M:sM]
The *statement was issued* by the State Department after clearance by President Eisenhower.

(159) [U.S.: others/R/M:sM]
All through the day the highest officials of the Government *had worked on an answer* to Premier Khrushchev's charges that the United States had been caught red-handed in an aerial-intelligence operation behind the Soviet borders.

(160) [U.S.: others/R/M:sM]
The statement *contained* what was probably *the first official admission* that extensive intelligence activities were being conducted along the Soviet frontiers.

(161) [U.S.: others/R/M:dM]
It *gave no assurance* that these activities would be curbed in the future.

(162) [U.S.: others/R/nM]
But it *justified* this intelligence work on several grounds.

(163) [U.S.: others/Q/M:dM]
"The Soviet Union", it *pointed out*, "has not been lagging behind in this field".

(164) [U.S.: others/R/nM]
Furthermore, it *said*, the excessive secrecy practiced by the Russians and their refusal to accept a United States plan for mutual protection against surprise attack obliged the free world to take every precaution.

(165) [U.S.: others/Q/nM]
"It is in relation to the danger of surprise attack that planes of the type of the unarmed civilian U-2 aircraft have made flights along the frontiers of the free world for the past four years", the statement *said*.

(166) [U.S.: others/R/nM]
It *did not repeat* the original explanation of the plane incident issued here Thursday by the National Aeronautical and Space Agency.

(167) [U.S.: others/R/nM]
The agency *said* the American pilot had last reported difficulty with his oxygen supply and *suggested* that he might have strayed over the Soviet frontier by inadvertence.

(168) [U.S.: others/sQ/nM]
Asked about the space agency's statement, officials *replied* with some embarrassment that "it was issued in complete good faith".

(169) [U.S.: others/R/nM]
They *said*, however, that they did not know whether the story of oxygen failure was true and that they did not know what officer or official outside Washington had authorized the flight.

(170) [U.S.: others/Q/nM]
Asked whether the pilot had been engaged on a mission for the space agency, as stated officially on Thursday, one official *replied*, "Obviously not."

(171) [U.S.S.R.: K/R/M:sM]
President Khrushchev's *sensational speech shattered the calm* of this hesitant spring day in the capital.

(172) [U.S.: others/R/M:sM]
The *discussions led up to* one vital issue: Should the United States admit that one of its planes had penetrated Soviet territory on an intelligence mission?

(173) [U.S.: others/R/M:sM]
A *determined argument was made by* some high officials that the United States should concede nothing.

(174) [U.S.: others/R/nM]
On the other hand, some officials *were reported to have argued* that it would be better to make some kind of avowal, to give a justification for what was being done and to state that the flight of the U-2 into Soviet territory had not been authorized in Washington.

(175) [U.S.: others/R/M:sM]
By stressing this lack of authorization, it *was apparently contended*, the good faith of President Eisenhower would be safeguarded.

COMMENTS:

Not only does the distribution of metapragmatic description types in Article 9 (dealing with new Soviet revelations) come a little closer to that observed in articles dealing with the earlier American account of the event (as shown in 4.3.1.). In addition, the distribution of metapragmatic description types in Article 10 is very similar to that discovered in previous texts about the

Soviets' story. Thus semi-quotes are patently used to dissociate the reporter from some crucial phrasings of American messages: 'probably' in (154), the claim that 'there was no authorization for any such flight' in (155), and the statement that the space agency's statement 'was issued in complete good faith' in (168).

Though Soviet espionage is presented as a fact (cf. the dead metaphor *pointed out* in (163), already discussed in 4.1.1.), though justifications for spying missions are not repudiated, and though the speculations that the Soviets might want to use the incident to their advantage at the Paris summit are certainly not contradicted, Article 10 counterbalances the implications of Article 9. The U.S. government's duplicity, though not stated as a fact, is offered as a distinct possibility. Consider the report that "All through the day the highest officials of the Government *had worked on an answer* to Premier Khrushchev's charges" (in (159)). The 'work' metaphor implies that the answer was far from being spontaneous. The lack of spontaneity is further elaborated by presenting details of the *discussion* that *led up to* the issue as to whether the U.S. should admit that one of its planes had penetrated Soviet territory on an intelligence mission (see (172)). The author does not vacillate about the fact of the mission. Within a context where governments traditionally refuse to comment on matters of espionage, officials are said to disagree as to whether they should break that tradition by speaking the truth or not: *a determined argument was made* against (in (173)); some *argued* that they should, while justifying the action but denying Washington's authorization of the flight (in (174)), and *contended* (a general conflict metaphor) that this would safeguard the President's good faith (in (175)). By sketching this background, the author opens the possibility that earlier official statements were not mistakes but intended fabrications. Moreover, this also presents the new statement as a calculated strategical move, thus casting doubt even on the denied involvement of President Eisenhower himself. Such doubt explains the semi-quotational treatment of 'there was no authorization for any such flight' in (155) and the emphatic report that officials *refused to comment* as to who might have authorized the flight (in (156)) — implying that they could have, but simply did not want to.

4.3.3. *Article 11 (front page)*

TITLE: Intelligence acts *admitted* by U.S. [U.S.: others/R/M:dM]
SUBTITLE: Both Soviet and American efforts in field *cited* in statement on plane. [U.S.: others/R/nM]

DATA AND COMMENTS

AUTHOR: Jack Raymond.
CONTENTS: Comments on the latests U.S. government-statement in the light of intelligence activities along the Soviet borders which are now officially admitted for the first time but which are also said to be very similar to those undertaken by the Soviets. Examples of such activities, both on the American and Soviet sides, are given. The Air Force's vagueness about some of the details of the latest incident and earlier clashes are speculated about.

METAPRAGMATIC DESCRIPTIONS:

(176) [U.S.: others/R/M:sM]
The United States statement today on the plane downed in the Soviet Union *contained the first official Government disclosure* that this country was engaged in aerial intelligence efforts.

(177) [U.S.: others/R/nM]
Heretofore such activities *have* only *been hinted at* through announcements of Soviet activities and military strength.

(178) [U.S.: others/sQ/nM]
The State Department's announcement *called attention to* both the United States' own intelligence-gathering efforts and those of the Soviet Union, saying that these are "certainly no secret".

(179) [U.S.: others/R/M:sM]
Officials today *would not amend the story they issued* at that time [in 1958] that the Air Force C-130, which was downed by the Russians, had accidently flown over the Soviet border.

(180) [U.S.: E/R/nM]
President Eisenhower *hinted* then that the Soviet Union might have lured the Air Force craft over Soviet territory with a false radio signal.

(181) [U.S.: others/R/nM]
The intelligence activities, as the State Department *noted*, have not been one-sided by any means.

(182) [U.S.: others/R/nM]
The chief difference in the two countries' activities, it has been *noted*, is that the United States has not yet had occasion to down a Soviet plane over its own or allied territory.

(183) [U.S.: others/R/M:sM]
At the Pentagon, officials *do not take a defensive attitude* about the many bases that the United States has established to ring the Soviet Union and other Communist countries.

(184) [U.S.: others/R/M:dM]
They *have attributed* the development of these bases to aggressive actions of the Soviet Union in the post-World War II period.

(185) [U.S.: others/R/nM]
Pentagon officials also *insist* that there is less need for espionage by a potential enemy in the United States where so many government activities are conducted in the open, than in the Soviet Union.

(186) [U.S.: others/R/nM]
In that connection [i.e. in connection with the latest incident], the Air Force *identified* Col. W. Shelton, described by Premier K. as the espionage superior of the pilot, as the commander of the Second Weather Reconnaissance Squadron (Provisional), stationed at Adana, in support of the N.A.S.A. research program.

(187) [U.S.: others/R/nM]
There *was no immediate comment available* from the Air force as to whether this would tend to confirm Mr. Khrushchev's charges, since the N.A.S.A. program in Turkey appeared to have been revealed as an intelligence operation.

(188) [U.S.: others/R/nM]
An Air Force spokesman *explained* that the term "provisional" indicated that the squadron was a special unit and not self-supporting logistically as were other Air Force units of its type.

(189) [U.S.: others/R/nM]
The spokesman *added* that the Air Force was puzzled by Premier Khrushchev's reference to "10-10" as the serial number of the alleged espionage unit.

(190) [U.S.: others/sQ/M:dM]
It [the U-2] *has been dubbed* a "sniffer."

(191) [U.S.: others/sQ/nM]
This plane *has* also *been described as* a "flying test bed" and details of its characteristics and the equipment it carries normally have been heavily classified.

(192) [U.S.: others/R/nM]
Among these instruments, N.A.S.A. officials had *noted*, was a 70-mm. camera.

(193) [U.S.: others/R/nM]
But this was intended to take pictures of cloud cover and of star formations, these officials *insisted*.

(194) [U.S.: others/R/nM]
There *was by no means any confirmation* today that all United States aircraft involved in these clashes [over the past 10 years] had been engaged in intelligence work.

COMMENTS:

The final sentence of this article, immediately following (194), says: "However, the contradiction between today's story of the latest incident and the one put out earlier appeared to confirm long-held speculations about them." This statement corroborates the suggestion (clearly present in Article 10) of large-scale fabrications. It is further supported by the author's semi-quotational dissociation from misleading Air Force euphemisms for the U-2 as a 'sniffer' (in (190)) and 'a flying test bed' (in (191)). Further, the metaphor chosen to report that officials *would not amend the story they issued* in connection with an incident with an Air Force C-130 in 1958 (see (179)) implies that, in the light of the recent events, that story might need mending. And the claim that Pentagon officials *do not take a defensive attitude* (in (183)) suggests that they can be criticized (or, to maintain the metaphor: 'attacked') though they themselves regard their activities as in line with the routine demands of their job.

4.3.4. *Further comments*

A few more related texts appeared in this issue of *The New York Times*: (i) "London troubled", subtitled "Fears that U.S. stance for summit parley will be injured". In this article, diplomats are said to be worried that Washington's position at the Paris summit will be considerably weakened by the incident, especially because of 'the first hasty denial of spying' and 'the subsequent admission forced from the Eisenhower Administration':

> "At first, Allied diplomats thought the Soviet version would be accepted only by the Left-Wing circles, neutralists and pacifists of Europe, Asia and Africa.
> The State Department's later acknowledgment of the nature of the mission, *even though it was unauthorized by the authorities in Washington* [emphasis mine; note the implication of factual truth], means that distrust of the United States will spread beyond those circles."

The incident is said to be called 'bad luck'. But Eisenhower's image is seen as seriously damaged, especially by the claim that he did not know about the flight.
(ii) "Excerpts from Premier Khrushchev's remarks on U.S. jet downed in Soviet."
(iii) "Text of the U.S. statement on plane."
(iv) "Downed U.S. pilot fell in love with flying on plane ride at 14."

The general picture emerging from this day's reporting is critical of the U.S. However, criticism of the Soviet Union is expressed in the same breath. And Article 9 was said to show a pattern of metapragmatic reporting on Khrushchev's disclosures which diverts the attention from American deceitfulness. Supporting this diversion is an indirectly related note entitled "Soviet moves decried" in which a study is cited branding the Soviet coexistence drive as 'a sleeping pill'. And a note "C.I.A. network praised", subtitled "Intelligence ring in Soviet described as effective", emphasizes the need — as seen by the C.I.A.'s inspector general — for even more effective intelligence, thus

		Eisenhower									others								
		Q			sQ			R			Q			sQ			R		
		nM	M		nM	M		nM	M		nM	M		nM	M		nM	M	
			dM	sM		dM	sM		dM	sM		dM	sM		dM	sM		dM	sM
May 6th	1. J. Raymond							1			1			3	1	1	14	1	
	2. O. Caruthers																1	1	
	3. W.J. Jorden										1			2			11	2	4
	4. Unsigned																1		
	5. Unsigned																		
May 7th	6. W.J. Jorden																5		1
	7. J. Raymond													5			17		
	8. M. Frankel																3		
May 8th	9. O. Caruthers																2	1	
	10. J. Reston										3	1		2	1		9	1	6
	11. J. Raymond							1						3			14	3	3

Table 1. May 6th-8th, U.S.

		Khrushchev								others							
		Q			sQ			R			Q			sQ			R		
		nM	dM (M)	sM (M)	nM	dM (M)	sM (M)	nM	dM (M)	sM (M)	nM	dM (M)	sM (M)	nM	dM (M)	sM (M)	nM	dM (M)	sM (M)
May 6th	1. J. Raymond			1	1			1									2		
	2. O. Caruthers				5	2	2	8	1	2									
	3. W.J. Jorden													1					
	4. Unsigned							1	1					1			2		
	5. Unsigned																		
May 7th	6. W.J. Jorden										1								
	7. J. Raymond							1		1				1			2		
	8. M. Frankel				2			2						5	1		8	2	
	9. O. Caruthers	3	1		3	1	1	18	1	2				1		2		1	1
May 8th	10. J. Reston									1									
	11. J. Raymond																		

Table 2. May 6th-8th, U.S.S.R.

indirectly lending support to the justification for the U-2 flight.

The distribution of the various types of metapragmatic descriptions, as documented and commented upon in the foregoing sections, is summarized in Tables 1 and 2. Since no dramatic changes take place in the functional principles underlying the distribution and its fluctuations, we can now start to comment more selectively on the metapragmatic metaphors used in the remainder of the corpus.

4.4. May 9th

On this second day after the official admission of spying, the reporting centers around (i) Khrushchev's revelations of some more details about the capture of the pilot, (ii) further speculations about the effects of the incident on the Paris summit and how Khrushchev could exploit it, (iii) Washington's profound sense of humiliation and its attempt to rescue the summit, (iv) the upset public opinion and the expectation of a congressional inquiry, and (v) the general dilemmas of intelligence. The following articles appeared in *The New York Times*:

ARTICLE 12 (front page), by Max Frankel, and sharing a title with Article 13, viz. "President sees Herter in effort to lessen blow to summit talks; Soviet *exploits* plane espionage" [U.S.S.R.: others/R/M:sM], subtitled "Moscow *is bitter*" [U.S.S.R.: others/R/M:sM] and sub-subtitled "Pilot becoming focus of criticism of U.S. — New *data given*" [U.S.S.R.: others/R/M:dM].

ARTICLE 13 (front page), by James Reston, under the same general title as Article 12, subtitled "Flights stopped", sub-subtitled "Washington is upset and humiliated by spy developments".

ARTICLE 14 (front page), by Dana Adams Schmidt: "Angry congressmen *urge* inquiry on spying activity" [U.S.: others/R/nM], subtitled "They *demand explanation* why flight was made just before summit — Need for such operations seen" [U.S.: others/R/nM]. Most of the demands reported in this article were predicated on the assumption that President Eisenhower had indeed not been informed of the flight.

ARTICLE 15 (front page), under the heading 'News analysis', by Hanson W. Baldwin: "Intelligence and survival", subtitled "Plane incident points up the dilemma involved in missions for information". From the properties of the U-2 it is inferred that, in the light of the recent equivocal admissions, it was probably the most successful reconnaissance plane ever built (immune to interception by fighter planes and, until the incident, outside the reach of Soviet ground-to-air defenses), so that its operations must have been closely directed by Washington.

A number of directly related articles are also included:
(i) "Europe dismayed by plane incident", subtitled "Serious concern is evident despite official silence".
(ii) "Many here decry timing of flight", subtitled "But test of opinion also finds support for mission", on American public opinion.
(iii) "Humphrey is critical".
(iv) "Kennedy scores Khrushchev", a note reporting Kennedy as having described Khrushchev's attitude as 'extreme, belligerent and menacing'.
(v) "Peiping assails U.S." on a Chinese reaction.
(vi) "Turkey denies acquiescence" on Turkey's disclaiming of responsibility.
(vii) "Pakistan plans protest to U.S. if plane flew from Peshawar."
(viii) "U.S. spy satellite planned for Fall", subtitled "Mission of Samos is to take photographs of every inch of communist territory".
(ix) "Soviet spy cases in U.S. recalled".
(x) "Intelligence lag often laid to U.S.", subtitled "Many critics have charged inadequacy of efforts to obtain foreign secrets".

Russians and Americans are attributed similar emotions in this day's reporting. Consider the following elaborate metapragmatic metaphors:

(195) (Article 12) [U.S.S.R.: others/R/M:sM]
The Russians already *are reacting with various expressions of injury and disappointment*.

(196) (Article 14) [U.S.: others/R/M:sM]
Anger, dismay and demands for investigation marked Congressional reaction today *to* the State Department's admission that the United States aircraft shot down by the Soviet Union had been on an intelligence-gathering mission.

The feelings are prominent enough for them to be expressed even in the subtitle and title of the respective articles.

Also deviousness is imputed to both. On the Soviet side, the metaphor of 'exploitation' is used to account for this, as in the shared title of Articles 12 and 13 and in (197).

(197) (Article 15) [U.S.S.R.: K/R/M:sM]
(The capture of Francis G. Powers [...] gave Premier Khrushchev an important political and psychological advantage just prior to the East-West summit conference.) It was an advantage the Soviet leader was quick to *exploit*.

That the 'exploitation' is a matter of interpretation rather than a directly observable fact gets somewhat blurred by metaphors such as the one in (198), with its source domain in a world of visible transactions.

> (198) (Article 12) [U.S.S.R.: others/R/M:dM]
> The Soviet Government *gave indications* today that the capture of an American reconnaissance flier deep inside Soviet territory last Sunday would become the focus of a major campaign to embarrass the West on the eve of the summit conference.

On occasion, American duplicity is slightly palliated by presenting the U.S. Government as the victim of Soviet scheming. In this context, one of the rare creative metaphors (significantly used in a 'News analysis' rather than in a regular report) can be cited:

> (199) (Article 15) [U.S.: others/R/M:cM]
> The United States Government, many members of Congress and much of the press *had been mouse-trapped into premature denials*.

The 'mouse-trap' metaphor should be clear. Less obvious are the implications of *premature*, which suggests that the *denials* themselves were not so terrible but that they were poorly planned. Yet the author agrees that they were 'incomplete lies', though he attributes these words to Khrushchev, drawing attention to his style, using the metaphor of 'bluntness':

> (200) (Article 15) [U.S.S.R.: K/sQ/M:sM]
> Mr. Khrushchev was able to show — with the capture of the pilot — that these were, *as he bluntly put it*, "complete lies."

In general, accusations against the U.S. government are phrased more mildly, as in (201) and (202).

> (201) (Article 15) [U.S.: others/sQ/M:sM]
> Saturday's *somewhat equivocal* United States *statement*, probably *deliberately cloudy* on this point [the issue of authorization from Washington], *declared that* "in so far as the authorities are concerned, there was no authorization for any such flights as described by Mr. Khrushchev."

> (202) (Article 13) [U.S.: others/R/M:sM]
> It [Washington] was depressed and humiliated by the United States' having been caught spying over the Soviet Union and trying to *cover up* its activities *in a series of misleading official announcements*.

But such phrasings are accompanied by an unwavering critical stance — not so much against the fact of espionage (except for the timing of the abortive flight) but against the government announcements. This is particularly clear in Article 13, authored by James Reston. It is clear that he includes the government's last statement within the scope its its *misleading official announce-*

ments. He claims emphatically that the fact of such flights must have been known widely in the administration, though not necessarily the fact of this individual mission. He widens the issue to the traditional disregard for truth in CIA statements, and argues for more thorough discussion of intelligence practices to dispel the impression that only the Soviet Union would resort to 'the black arts in diplomacy'.

4.5. May 10th to May 12th

The tone of the reporting does not change significantly on May 10th and May 11th. But the topic shifts to Khrushchev's warning that the Soviets would attack bases used by U.S. spying planes (in the May 10 issue), and a subsequent U.S. vow that it would defend its allies if bases were to be attacked (in the May 11 issue). In addition, the need to spy on the Soviet Union gets more heavily emhasized, and flights over Soviet territory are now openly declared to have been undertaken since 1956. By doing so, Soviet defense weakness is indicated. Doubt in cast on whether the U-2 was indeed *shot* down.

The May 12 issue of *The New York Times* carries the first report of direct statements by President Esenhower about the incident, made during a news conference:

ARTICLE 16 (front page)
TITLE: Khrushchev cools to President, doubts welcome on Soviet visit; Eisenhower *defends* espionage. [U.S.: E/R/M:sM]
(Note: this title also covers a report on the 'clouded outlook' for the summit and one on Khrushchev's expression of disappointment in Eisenhower himself while he was visiting the 'plane exhibit' organized in Moscow)
SUBTITLE: President *asserts* secrecy of Soviet justifies spying. [U.S.: E/R/nM]
SUB-SUBTITLE: *Stresses* ability of Russians to prepare surprise attack — He *expresses no regret* over plane episode. [U.S.: E/R/nM] + [U.S.: E/R/M:dM]
AUTHOR: Felix Belair Jr.

The surface distribution of metapragmatic description types in this article is very similar to the functional distribution observed in reports on Khrushchev's announcements. Reported speech governed by non-metaphorical LAVs predominates, but also semi-quotes are frequent, as in (203).

(203) [U.S.: E/sQ/nM]
President Eisenhower *said* tonight that the Soviet Union's ability to prepare in secret a massive surprise attack was ample warrant for the United States' "distasteful but vital" espionage activities.

But whereas metapragmatic metaphors were resorted to in order to underscore the emotionality, hostility and bad manners of Khrushchev's communicative behavior, with reference to President Eisenhower metapragmatic metaphors (except for the 'defense' metaphor in the title of Article 16) come into play to indicate emotionlessness, rationality, and a quiet — though firm — manner of speaking. Just consider (204) and (205).

(204) [U.S.: E/sQ/M:dM]
In a carefully worded statement read at his news conference the President *said* that the Soviet "fetish of secrecy and concealment" was "a major cause of international tension and uneasiness."

(205) [U.S.: E/sQ/M:sM]
There was neither regret nor apology in President Eisenhower's *statement* of the case nor in the firm, measured tones with which he read it.

The main piece of new information in Eisenhower's message was that he "assumed personal responsibility for the directives since the beginning of his Administration on the gathering of information necessary to protect the United States and the free world against surprise attack and to enable them to make effective preparations for defense." Eisenhower also expressed the hope that the summit meeting in Paris could still contribute to a relaxation of tensions. Meanwhile, Khrushchev is reported to have said that he was 'horrified' to learn that President Eisenhower himself had approved espionage flights.

4.6. May 13th to May 16th

On May 13th, *The New York Times* reports on a U.S. note delivered to the Soviet Government, in which the 'aggressive intent' of the U-2 flights is disclaimed and an attempt is made to dispel the thought that the mission two weeks before the summit had been intended to poison U.S.-Soviet relations.

On May 14th, an order to all government officials to stop talking in public about the U-2 is reported.

In the May 15 issue, Khrushchev is said to have arrived in Paris, 'glum and reserved', but apparently in a milder mood than expected:

(206) [U.S.S.R.: K/R/M:sM]
(Premier Khrushchev arrived here today looking as glum as the Moscow skies he had left behind.) But *his first words* at Orly Airport *were mild and unprovocative*.

DATA AND COMMENTS 83

The absence of provocative remarks upon arrival is said to have raised hopes for the summit.

The next day, May 16th, *The New York Times* describes renewed pessimism on the eve of the summit (to be opened on the 16th), resulting from a 'trading of snubs' between Eisenhower and Khrushchev:

(207) (frontpage title) [U.S.: E/R/M:sM]
President in Paris *trades snubs with* Khrushchev.

(208) [U.S.: E/R/M:sM] + [U.S.S.R.: K/R/M:sM]
An atmosphere of renewed pessimism, following yesterday's brief assertions of hope, was created by *snubs administered* by President Eisenhower and Premier Khrushchev, and by the impression of toughness left by Mr. Khrushchev in his first diplomatic contacts here.

(209) [U.S.S.R.: K/R/M:sM]
Mr. Khrushchev's snub was his lack of any effort to *seek an advance meeting* with General Eisenhower.

(210) [U.S.: E/R/M:sM]
(On his side, the President, in an arrival statement at Orly Airfield at 9:30 A.M., expressed pleasure at the opportunity to meet again with General de Gaulle, Macmillan and Chancellor Adenauer of West Germany.) He *pointedly omitted* any such reference to Mr. Khrushchev.

Apart from such details, there were few clues as to the attitudes of both leaders, and the reporting centers around quoted expectations and speculations.

The U-2 episode in Soviet-American communication reaches its climax on the opening day of the summit. Therefore, the May 17 issue of *The New York Times* will again be dealt with more fully.

4.7. May 17th

4.7.1. *Article 17 (front page)*

TITLE: U.S.-Soviet *clash* disrupts summit talks [U.S.: E/R/M:sM] + [U.S.S.R.: K/R/M:sM]; Khrushchev *cancels* Eisenhower's visit [U.S.S.R.: K/R/nM]; U-2 spy flights ended, President *reveals* [U.S.: E/R/M:dM].
SUBTITLE: *Harsh exchange.* [U.S.: E/R/M:sM] + [U.S.S.R.: K/R/M:sM]
SUB-SUBTITLE: Russian *asks* parley be postponed for 6 to 8 months. [U.S.S.R.: K/R/nM]
AUTHOR: Drew Middleton
CONTENTS: Khrushchev is reported to have demanded (i) condemnation of the U-2 flights, (ii) their immediate cancelling, (iii) punishment of those responsible. Otherwise the summit would have to be postponed for 6 to 8

months, i.e. until after the American elections. Macmillan's and de Gaulle's attempts to make him change his mind are said to have been rather unsuccessful. Speculations about internal Soviet pressure on Mr. Khrushchev are presented.

METAPRAGMATIC DESCRIPTIONS:

(211) [U.S.: E/R/M:dM] + [U.S.S.R.: K/R/M:dM]
The summit conference suffered an apparently mortal blow at its opening session today when Premier Khrushchev and President Eisenhower *exchanged charges* that blighted hopes for an early relaxation of tension between East and West.

(212) [U.S.S.R.: K/R/M:sM]
The Soviet Premier *bluntly told* the United States President that he would not be welcome if he went to the Soviet Union on his proposed visit next month.

(213) [U.S.S.R.: K/R/M:dM]
The Soviet Government is convinced, Mr. Khrushchev *continued*, that the next United States Administration, or even the one after that, will understand that there is no other course but peaceful coexistence with the Soviet Union.

(214) [U.S.S.R.: K/sQ/nM]
There is "no better way out" of the dispute arising from the United States intelligence flights over Soviet territory, the Premier *said*, than to postpone the conference for six to eight months.

(215) [U.S.S.R.: K/R/M:sM]
At the end of *his blistering speech*, the system of high-level consultation and negotation seemed *wrecked*.

(216) [U.S.S.R.: K/R/nM]
Mr. Khrushchev *demanded* that President Eisenhower fulfill three conditions if there were to be summit talks.

(217) [U.S.S.R.: K/R/M:dM]
His demands *followed a tirade against* the United States for having sent U-2 photoreconnaissance planes over the Soviet Union.

(218) [U.S.: E/R/M:sM]
President Eisenhower *met* one demand only.

(219) [U.S.: E/sQ/nM]
He *announced* that the flights had been suspended after the recent incident "and are not to be resumed."

(220) [U.S.: E/sQ/nM]
The President also *said* he planned, in the event an accord with the Soviet Union on the subject proved impossible, to submit to the United Nations a proposal for "aerial surveillance to detect preparations for attack."

DATA AND COMMENTS

(221) [U.S.S.R.: K/sQ/nM]
These moves failed to satisfy Mr. Khrushchev, who *had demanded* first, condemnation of "inadmissible provocative actions" on the part of the United States Air Force, second a ban on flights now and in the future and, finally, United States punishment of those "directly guilty" of "deliberate violation of the Soviet Union."

(222) [U.S.S.R.: K/sQ/nM]
The Soviet leader *remarked* at the end of the disastrous session that he would be "happy" to spend a day or two strolling under the chestnut trees.

(223) [U.S.S.R.: K/R/nM]
But Mr. Khrushchev still *was demanding* more than the President appeared willing to give.

(224) [U.S.S.R.: others/R/nM]
A high Soviet official *declared* his Government did not believe the President's statement to the conference had met Mr. Khrushchev's conditions.

(225) [U.S.S.R.: others/sQ/nM]
Georgi A. Zhukov, head of the State Committee for Cultural Relations With Foreign Countries, *said* the Premier was "still waiting for a reply" to his demands.

(226) [U.S.S.R.: others/sQ/nM]
The Eisenhower statement ending espionage flights was "canceled out", Mr. Zhukov *said*, by a single line in the speech.

(227) [U.S.: E/sQ/nM]
This was the President's *remark that* actual United States statements were not threats but only declarations "that go no further than to say that the United States will not shirk its responsibility to safeguard against surprise attack."

(228) [U.S.S.R.: K/R/M:sM]
Mr. Khrushchev's *speech was a devastating and explosive performance.*

(229) [U.S.S.R.: K/R/M:sM]
His denunciation of the United States and his imposition of conditions *were capped by his brutally frank announcement that* in the circumstances General Eisenhower's visit must be postponed.

(230) [U.S.: E/sQ/M:sM]
President Eisenhower *thought* Premier Khrushchev's speech, as bitter as any made at the height of the "cold war", showed he had come to Paris intending to "wreck" the conference.

(231) [U.S.S.R.: K/R/M:sM]
President de Gaulle made a speech of welcome and then Premier Khrushchev *embarked on his tirade.*

(232) [U.S.: E/R/nM]
President Eisenhower *responded in* what Prime Minister Macmillan described afterward as *a "statesmanlike and restrained manner".*

(233) [U.S.S.R.: K/R/M:dM]
The Soviet leader *made the admission*, without precedent in Mr. Bohlen's long experience, that the issue of the United States flights was deeply involved with the internal policies of the Soviet Union.

(234) [U.S.: others/R/M:sM]
This appeared to confirm *persistent reports that* the shooting down of the United States plane had exacerbated the opposition to Mr. Khrushchev's détente policy that had been developing in the army and among Communist party fundamentalists.

(235) [U.S.S.R.: K/R/M:cM]
Some form of internal pressure may have compelled the Premier to come to Paris and *explode his land mine under the conference*, British diplomats said.

(236) [U.S.S.R.: K/R/nM]
Mr. Khrushchev also *refused* General Eisenhower's offer of direct talks on the flights over Soviet territory.

(237) [U.S.S.R.: K/Q/nM]
Later, Mr. Khrushchev, responding to the suggestion that the Soviet Union also engaged in espionage, raised his clubby arms and *declaimed*, "As God is my witness, my hands are clean and my soul is pure!"

(238) [U.S.: others/R/nM]
The watchful Mr. Bohlen *noted* that Mr. Khrushchev seemed to pay a great deal of attention during the meeting to his two chief aides, Marshal Rodion Y. Malinovsky, Minister of Defense, and Andrei A. Gromyko, Foreign Minister.

4.7.2. Article 18 (front page)

Under the heading "News analysis".
TITLE: Conflict at the summit.
SUBTITLE: A view that Khrushchev's attack may presage a new Berlin crisis.
AUTHOR: James Reston
CONTENTS: The diplomatic world in Paris is said to have been shocked by what they feel was a major failure of diplomacy on the part of Premier Khrushchev: whereas they started the day with criticism of Eisenhower's clumsy handling of the U-2 affair, they ended it with sympathy for him. Strong Soviet pressure on Khrushchev is hypothesized as the cause of the 'blunder'. There are speculations that Khrushchev was preparing the summit participants for a tough stand on the Berlin issue, imposed on him by his colleagues at the Kremlin: "No doubt this [Eisenhower's responsibility for spying] did surprise and disappoint the Soviet leader. But the feeling here is that, more important, it provided just the incident that was needed to give the opponents of Mr. Khrushchev's policy the upper hand." On this view, the

incident in Paris was just a preliminary to a more serious crisis over Berlin.

METAPRAGMATIC DESCRIPTIONS:

(239) [U.S.S.R.: K/sQ/M:sM]
Nikita S. Khrushchev, Premier of the Soviet Union, had *leveled a charge* of "treachery" against the President of the United States.

(240) [U.S.S.R.: K/R/nM]
He *had demanded* that the Government of the United States apologize to the Soviet Union for having sent planes over Soviet territory, promise never to do it again and punish the persons responsible.

(241) [U.S.S.R.: K/R/M:dM]
In short, Mr. Khrushchev *brought up* almost everything but "the lynchings in the South" and *insisted* that unless the President cried "uncle" the Soviet Union could not negotiate with such a country.

(242) [U.S.S.R.: K/R/M:cM]
The reaction of a few experienced and detached diplomats who *were not blown over* by Mr. Khrushchev's *storm* was that there was an enormous difference [between what was 'news' and what was 'truth'].

(243) [U.S.S.R.: K/R/M:dM] + [U.S.: E/R/nM]
In the first place, while it was "news" that Mr. Khrushchev *had presented* what President Eisenhower called an "ultimatum" that there be no more flights over the Soviet Union, the actual fact was that President Eisenhower *had reassured* Mr. Khrushchev that the sky-spy flights had been grounded and Mr. Khrushchev knew it.

(244) [U.S.S.R.: K/sQ/nM] + [U.S.S.R.: others/R/nM]
Second, while Mr. Khrushchev *said* that his country could not "be among the participants in negotiation where one of them [the United States] has made treachery the basis of his policy", his subordinates were running all over the Palais Chaillot tonight *saying* that of course the Soviet Union did not mean to break off negotiations in Geneva with those Americans who were engaged in the talks on disarmament and the suspension of nuclear weapons testing.

(245) [U.S.S.R.: others/R/nM]
Third, these Soviet officials were also *saying* that while President Eisenhower had really been very irresponsible in the spy plane case, and was not wanted as a visitor in Moscow, actually he was a pleasant man who had merely come close to the end of his term and therefore had no authority to negotiate big issues.

(246) [U.S.S.R.: K/R/M:sM]
Mr. Khrushchev's *savage attack was responsible for* this transformation [from criticism directed against Eisenhower to sympathy for him].

(247) [U.S.S.R.: K/R/M:cM] + [U.S.S.R.: others/R/M:sM]
After Mr. Khrushchev *threw out his thunderbolt* at the Elysée Palace this morning, his assistants *were at great pains to explain* to reporters that this did not mean that the Soviet Union was now prepared to create a new and larger crisis by making a separate peace treaty with the Communist East German Government.

4.7.3. Related articles

ARTICLE 19 (front page), by William J. Jorden: "Ending of flights surprises capital", subtitled "Eisenhower policy viewed by many as shift — Nixon remark *cited*" [U.S.: others/R/nM]. Eisenhower's announcement that surveillance flights over Soviet territory would be stopped, is reported to have taken official Washington by surprise, especially since the flights had been so ardently defended as a matter of necessary information gathering on previous days.

ARTICLE 20 (front page), by Russell Baker: "Capital angered", subtitled "Both parties *condemn* 'insult' as a plot to wreck conference" [U.S.: others/sQ/nM]. Reactions in Washington are described. Some politicians such as Adlai Stevenson are said to have expressed criticism of the Administration's 'mishandling' of the incident:

(248) [U.S.: others/Q/nM]
"To first deny and then admit the flight over Russian territory, and to suggest that they would also continue, left Mr. Khrushchev no choice but to protest," Mr. Stevenson *said*. "He could hardly ignore these threats to continue to violate Soviet air space and preserve his leadership at home."

But leaders of both parties voice their anger over Khrushchev's 'insult':

(249) [U.S.: others/R/M:sM]
On the Senate floor members of both parties *angrily denounced* the Soviet leader *in unusually tough language* for what was everywhere regarded as a calculated insult aimed at wrecking the summit conference.

Further, this article reports speculations about the effects of the incident on the approaching elections.

ARTICLE 21 (a four-sentence note tucked away on p. 15, unsigned): "President holds temper — until meeting is over."

(250) [U.S.: E/R/M:sM]
President Eisenhower *kept his temper in check* at today's summit conference meetings.

(251) [U.S.: E/R/M:sM]
But afterward in private *he exploded with fury* over Premier Khrushchev's tactics.

ARTICLE 22 (front page), by A.M. Rosenthal: "*Bitter propaganda exchanges* put summit split before the world" [U.S.: others/R/M:sM] + [U.S.S.R.: others/R/M:sM]. Report of how about 2,000 correspondents gathered in Paris were able to observe the events and were informed at ensuing news conferences.

ARTICLE 23 (front page), by Robert C. Doty: "Macmillan talks with Khrushchev", subtitled "Also meets with the Gaulle and Eisenhower in effort to save summit parley".

ARTICLE 24, by Max Frankel: "Russians *blame* West for crisis" [U.S.S.R.: others/R/nM], subtitled "Khruschev's *stern stand startles* envoys [U.S.S.R.: K/R/M:sM] — British press accuses Premier".

ARTICLE 25 (unsigned three-paragraph note on p. 17): "Order issued Thursday".

(252) [U.S.: E/R/M:dM]
President Eisenhower *issued orders* [...] last Thursday to halt the reconnaissance flights over the Soviet Union, informed sources said here today.

(253) [U.S.: others/R/nM]
The order *was not publicized*, the sources said, because the United States wanted to save the disclosure for the summit conference.

ARTICLE 26, by Harrison E. Salisbury (under the heading 'News analysis'): "Soviet policy shift", subtitled "Political and military forces discerned behind the harder line toward the West". Salisbury attributes the events to a 'quiet shift in the Kremlin balance of power' which 'has placed greater authority in the hands of military and political advocates of a harder line toward the West'.

The following additional materials were included in the May 17 issue of *The New York Times*:
(i) Texts of Khrushchev and Eisenhower statements on summit and the plane case.
(ii) Excerpts from news conference by Hagerty and Bohlen on summit parley.
(iii) "Khrushchev is blamed", on editorials in British papers.
(iv) "Father weighs trip", subtitled "Parent of U.S. pilot hopes to offer himself in son's place".
(v) "Russians assure West on Berlin", subtitled "Disclaim any plan to sign East German peace pact before a new summit".
(vi) "Soviet warns West on air intrusions in East Germany".
(vii) "Soviet again jamming broadcasts by 'Voice'".

4.7.4. Comments

Until May 16th, when the reciprocal administering of 'snubs' dominated the headlines, all reporting in *The New York Times* on Soviet or American comments pertaining to the U-2 and the resulting Soviet-American conflict concentrated on properties of the utterances produced and of their utterers. Quite naturally, the communicative *exchange* immediately becomes the real focus on May 17th, the first day after the opening of the summit meeting. This exchange is characterized as a *clash* (see the title of Article 17), as a *harsh exchange* (in the subtitle of the same article) and as a *bitter propaganda exchange* (in the title of Article 22).

So far so good. But the reporters' choice of metapragmatic metaphors to describe Khrushchev's and Eisenhower's respective verbal behavior singles out Khrushchev as the sole person responsible for those identified properties of the exchange. Thus, after de Gaulle's opening address, Khruschev *embarked on his tirade* (in (231)), a *savage attack* (in (246)) during which he *leveled a charge of 'treachery'* at Eisenhower (in (239)) and *bluntly told* him (in (212)) that he would not be welcome in Moscow unless Khrushchev's demands were met. This *brutally frank announcement* with which he *capped* his charges and demands (see (229)) was probably the *thunderbolt* which he *threw out* (in (247)) and the *land mine* which he *exploded under the conference* (in (235)). His *blistering speech* did not only *wreck* this particular summit meeting, but the whole 'system of high-level consultation and negotiation' (see (215)). All in all, his address was a *devastating and explosive performance* (in (228)). And only 'experienced and detached diplomats' *were not blown over by Mr. Khrushchev's storm* (in (242)).

On the other hand, though Eisenhower *exploded with fury* (in (251)) in private after the meeting, during the meeting he *kept his temper in check* (see 250) and *responded in a "statesmanlike and restrained manner"* (see (232)). British Prime Minister Macmillan is quoted saying that he thought his 'old friend' had "reacted with disregard for 'face' that one would not find in lesser men coming from lesser countries" (Article 17).

This description clearly places the burden of guilt on Khrushchev's shoulders. The reports show that this is how the events were interpreted. Motives for the Soviet leader's 'insults' and 'bad manners' are looked for only in speculations about pressure from his colleagues in the Politburo who did not like his policy of détente. The link with the fact of airspace violations, the President's involvement, and the earlier suggestion that U-2 missions would continue, is no longer emphasized, except in the quote from Stevenson (in Article 20, see (248)). In other words, it seemed perfectly justified that politicians back in Washington would *angrily denounce* the Soviet leader *in unusually tough language* (see (249)).

4.8. May 18th to May 20th

The general assessment of the incident (as described in section 4.7.4.) does not change during the following days.

On May 18th, democratic leaders in Washington are said to stand behind the President during the crisis, though they hint at a possible investigation of the 'blunders'. The summit conference is reported to have broken up in a dispute over Khrushchev's insisting on Eisenhower's apology for the U-2 flights. A major change in Soviet policy, a 'warmed-up cold war' is suggested. But one article (by Max Frankel), "No alternatives for Premier seen", subtitled "U.S. handling of U-2 issue is said to have dictated the course of events", presents the view of diplomats in Moscow that the Soviet Union's policies will not necessarily change, but that Khrushchev could not possibly have acted differently if he wanted to keep his people's support and sympathy. Especially the Soviet Union's desire to be recognized as the equal of the U.S. is said to have been greatly frustrated by suggestions in Washington that the espionage flights could be continued without their being able to do anything about it.

On May 19th, a news conference held by Khrushchev is the focus of reporting. His emotional and belligerent style is again heavily emphasized, as in (254).

(254) [U.S.S.R.: K/R/M:sM]
Premier Khrushchev resumed the "cold war" today with *a rolling barrage of threats, menaces and insults.*

Once again there are speculations about a power struggle in Moscow.

On May 20th, both Eisenhower and Khrushchev are reported to have left Paris (the former for Lisbon, the latter for Berlin). Stevenson is said to hold that the U.S. is to blame too; the subtitle of the article dealing with his claims: "Says it gave Soviet crowbar and sledgehammer with which to wreck parley". This formulation, of course, still leaves the heaviest burden of guilt on Khrushchev's shoulders.

5. A FUNCTIONAL ANALYSIS

5.0. Introduction

Our comments on the functional distribution of metapragmatic description types, and in particular on the use of metapragmatic metaphors, in the reporting by journalists of *The New York Times* on the U-2 incident and the resulting abortive summit in Paris in May 1960, have led to a range of observations about the framing of the incident as a political-communicative event. Some of these I want to summarize again before attempting any conclusions.

(i) On the first day after Khrushchev's announcement that an American plane had been shot down over Soviet territory, the metapragmatic framing of the events tends to indicate that reporters attach less credibility to the details of this announcement (according to which the plane had willfully violated Soviet air space for reasons of espionage) than to the official U.S. explanation that a N.A.S.A. weather-observation plane of the U-2 type might have strayed across the Turkish-Soviet border after having reported trouble with the oxygen equipment. This lower degree of credibility is partly established by the factual (content-centered) and detailed reporting of the explanation, and partly by the choice of LAVs focusing on Khrushchev's emotionality, hostility, and bad manners. Facing this attitude is a restrained American response.

(ii) On the second day, a new element is introduced: emotion-oriented descriptions of Khrushchev's utterances are framed in such a way as to suggest demagogical calculations behind them rather than expressive value. His revelations are presented as a pre-summit maneuver.

(iii) On the third day, after the U.S. admission of spying, details of Khrushchev's revelations are no longer cast in a doubt-provoking mold. But his style of message delivery becomes the focus (especially an aspect of exaggeration which underscores the possibility of manipulative intent), thus diverting the attention from the American fabrications on the previous days. These implications, however, are counterbalanced by an article by James Reston (Article 10) which clearly offers the U.S. government's duplicity as a distinct possibility (not only with respect to the first official statement, but even with reference to the new version disclaiming President Eisenhower's responsibility). This suggestion is further supported by the metapragmatic framing of U.S. statements in Article 11. (At the same time, the Soviet Union is beginning to get criticized for espionage activities of their own.)

(iv) In general, this picture is maintained until the summit in Paris. The main new fact is an announcement by President Eisenhower in which he takes full responsibility for the espionage activities. This message is metapragmatically provided with a frame of emotionlessness and rationality.

(v) The communicative exchange which constitutes the climax of the conflict is presented as a clash for which Khrushchev's hostile attitude and bad manners are held entirely responsible. Metapragmatic metaphors are heavily relied on to establish this impression.

In the light of the historical information now available to us, it is possible to make a serious evaluation of the performance of *The New York Times* in its reporting of the U-2 incident. One obvious standard of evaluation, *news value* or newsworthiness, can be taken for granted. Therefore, the following brief remarks will be restricted to matters of *truth* (in 5.1.), *interpretation* (in 5.2.), and *understanding* (in 5.3.).

5.1. News reporting and truth

As pointed out in chapter 2, any evaluation of the objectivity or truthfulness of news reports has to be established with reference to what reporters could reasonably be expected to have known at the time of writing. As far as this criterion is concerned, *The New York Times* performs rather poorly on May 6th and May 7th. U-2 flights had been a fact since 1956. The Soviets had already made charges to that effect in that same year, and news correspondents had been informed of those charges (see Charles E. Bohlen 1973: 464). Moreover, the fact of those flighs (not just of the Russian charges) could have been reasonably suspected on the basis of a series of otherwise hard-to-explain events which found their way into the news (see D. Wise and T.B Ross 1962: 53f.), and had been known beyond any doubt to editors and reporters of various newspapers such as the *Washington Post* and *The New York Times* well in advance of the incident (M. Schudson 1978: 172). One of them was James Reston of *The New York Times*, who had known about them for a year (see John Hohenberg 1978: 153). Ignoring the issue as to whether publication of the overflight story should have been withheld, motivated as it was by concern for the public interest, as seen by the press, "Whether or not the *Times* or any newspaper should have acquiesced in Eisenhower's lie is another matter entirely, particularly since the lie couldn't hold anyway." (T. Wicker 1975: 261) Acquiescence in a governmental lie certainly characterized the May 6 and May 7 reporting. Whose acquiescence it was, however, is not so clear. Did the individual reporters know about the flights? Maybe not. Note that the first one of James Reston's articles did not appear until May 8th and that he openly casts doubt even on details of the official admission of espionage in which Eisenhower's responsibility is disclaimed. Probably the acquiescence of the first two days was editorial policy inspired by a vague hope that a major incident could still be avoided, and maybe an even vaguer hope that Washington's official story would be true. If so, a similar pattern would emerge as in the reporting, 40 years earlier, of the events during the Russian Revolution (see section 1.2).

Whether one regards the withholding of information, under certain circumstances, as responsible or not, there are at least two bothersome aspects to it. First, as James Reston points out in Article 13, this policy certainly contributed to the impression in the public mind that dubious intelligence practices were mainly the province of the Soviet Union. Second, the editors could — and probably should, in the light of what they know — have prevented a framing of the communicative events biased against the credibility of the Soviet accusations.

But once the fact of espionage had been officially admitted — and defended — further stories tend to achieve a high degree of accuracy as to the 'objective' truth of the facts reported. Thus there was nothing untruthful about depicting Eisenhower's style as restrained and detached — the absolute antipode to Khrushchev's almost proverbial tirades. Khrushchev never was one to hide his emotions — to put it mildly. Thus it was probably an understatement when Khrushchev wrote in his memoirs (1970: 565), with reference to a Rumanian's suggestion for the Soviets to pull out their troops:

"I must confess that my initial reaction to his suggestion wasn't very sensible.
I would even go so far as to say I lost my temper."

Nor did he shy away from the use of strong and 'undiplomatic' language. Sentences such as "there are those who still quake before Stalin's dirty underwear" (1970: 2) or "Nowadays our military men are all dressed up like canaries" (1970: 525) seemed to come quite naturally to him. And to the extent that manners are concerned one could reasonably hold that they were pretty bad indeed. There is not only the well-known shoe-slamming at the United Nations in New York. Charles Bohlen (1973: 472) provides us with another illustration:

> "At a reception [in Moscow], Khrushchev began to shout at [U.S. Ambassador] Thompson about the U-2. To illustrate his point, he said, "Do you think it is all right to do this?" and stepped heavily on the Ambassador's foot. Afterwards, he told Thompson, "I didn't mean to hurt you.""

In other words, as far as the factual representation of events was concerned, the metaphors underscoring emotionality, expressiveness of hostility and bad manners, were probably well-chosen.

5.2. News reporting and interpretation

Also with respect to the interpretation as to why Khrushchev behaved the way he did, especially at the opening of the Paris summit, *The New York Times* can hardly be blamed. The explanations (found, e.g., in Articles 18, by James Reston, and 26, by Harrison Salisbury) based on speculations about a power struggle in the Kremlin between Khrushchev and those who thought he was too mild on the West, have since remained essentially unchanged. Khrushchev had held high hopes for the summit, founded on a fundamental sympathy towards Eisenhower. He had also expected Eisenhower's visit to Moscow to add to his own prestige at home. Therefore the anger and disappointment which he voiced in connection with the President's responsibility for the U-2 espionage missions were genuine. And at the same time the incident played into the hands of Khrushchev's political opponents who could now 'prove' that his confidence in a Western leader had been misplaced. As a result, he was most probably under pressure not to enter into negotiations in Paris unless he could squeeze a formal apology out of Eisenhower. His failed attempt to do so must have contributed to his ouster a few years later. This is George F. Kennan's analysis (1972: 143):

> "Time after time, as in Pakistan or Okinawa, the maintenance and development of military or air bases would be stubbornly pursued with no evidencee of any effort to balance this against the obvious political costs. Political interests would continue similarly to be sacrificed or placed in jeopardy by the avid and greedy pursuit of military intelligence; and when our failure to exercise any adequate restraint on such activities led, as it did through the U-2 episode, to the shattering of the political career of the only Soviet statesman of the post-Stalin period with whom we might conceivably have worked out a firmer sort of coexistence and to the replacement of his dominant influence by that of a coterie of military and police officials far more reactionary and militaristic in temper, there was only momentary embarrassment in Washington, no one was held to blame, and no one thought to conduct any serious investigation into the causes of so grievous an error of American national policy."

Also these wider policy issues were already raised, in a somewhat milder form, by drawing attention to the recklessness of a flight over Soviet territory just two weeks before a major diplomatic event.

5.3. News reporting and understanding

Going beyond an interpretation of Khrushchev's behavior in the immediate context of a newsworthy event to a real understanding of the Soviet sentiments and motives involved, seemed much harder to realize within the confines of the news reporting tradition. It is difficult to decide without further comparative investigations whether the tradition in general is to blame, or whether the nature of the communicative conflict to be reported (with Sd as a member of one of the participating nations) precluded a deeper analysis. Anyway, only one article (in the May 18 issue of *The New York Times*) probes into underlying motives which are said to be found in the Soviets' desire to be recognized as an equal to the United States. Thus the mere suggestion that the U-2 overflights could be continued without their being able to do anything about it, was about as insulting as spitting in their face. In such a context, a basic diplomatic failure on the part of the U.S. could have been pointed out (if understanding-oriented reports had been given more attention): a complete 'disregard for face', not in Prime Minister Macmillan's sense (see 4.7.4.), but in the sense of a disregard for the *Soviets'* face. From this point of view, it could have been shown, Khrushchev's demand for a formal apology was not at all unreasonable. Eisenhower's (unfortunately purely hypothetical) apology would not have implied a condemnation of all espionage activities. It would have served the function of any ordinary apology, a device to restore the addressee's 'face' after it has been threatened. The face-threatening activity in this case was the U.S. decision, as Khrushchev put it in one of his speeches, to simply open the Soviet skies for themselves after the Soviets had rejected an American 'open skies' proposal. It may not be a newspaper's task (not even in its editorials) to dictate a course of action. However, a further understanding-oriented analysis of the events could at least have demonstrated that Eisenhower's refusal to apologize was not the only (and maybe not the best) alternative available to him.

Note that the foregoing considerations are centered around the interpretation of a verbal action type. Unfortunately, *The New York Times'* lack of disagreement (or unexpressed agreement) with Eisenhower's understanding of the communicative value of an apology, is only symptomatic of the way in which communicative interaction in general is left behind at the level of objective reporting, without further attempts to open them interpretatively to the point of real understanding. As pointed out (in 5.1.), the metapragmatic framing of Khrushchev's and Eisenhower's verbal behavior does not violate standards of accuracy. However, it completely disregards the fact, usually not so much neglected where other types of human conduct are concerned, that the same surface activities (in this case utterances) may carry different weights in different societies. In particular, aspects of speaking style are presented as subject to universally valid norms. Though this universality is not asserted, it is heavily implied by neglecting to draw attention to variability. Thus, when Khrushchev is reported, quite accurately, to have 'exploded' in public, such behavior is likely to be judged by Hd (in this case the readership of *The New York Times*) in terms of his own culture-specific standards of behavior which dictate that explosions are permissible in private but not in public. Those standards shape the typically Western concept of diplomacy in which only unemotional, detached debating and negotiating is acceptable — irrespective of what one may feel. Therefore, Eisenhower is clearly evaluated as a 'real' diplomat because he *kept his temper in check* (see (250)), even though *he exploded with fury* (in (251)) in private, and though his emotions may have been visible in different ways during the meeting; in fact, Bohlen (1973: 468) notes that "As Khrushchev talked, Eisenhower's bald head turned various shades of pink, a sure sign that he was using every bit of will to hold his temper," adding that "When Eisenhower spoke, he gave no sign of the intense anger that he had obviously felt a few minutes before." Clearly, there is the sharpest possible contrast between a detached debating style and an openly antagonistic one. But the point is that the difference is *mainly a matter of style*. Unfortunately, it is a common Western presumption that the former is, by nature, superior to the latter[13]. That is why only Eisenhower is viewed as having behaved in a 'statesmanlike' fashion (see (232)) and why Macmillan is (approvingly) quoted saying that the President's reaction to Khrushchev's tirade at the summit was such as "one would not find in lesser men coming from lesser countries". The reporters' acquiescence in culture-specific visions of universally valid norms of verbal interaction, in terms of which 'objectively' reported exchanges are likely to be interpreted, may contribute to serious misunderstandings. In this case it is at least partly responsible for the possibility of viewing Khrushchev as entirely responsible for the failure of the summit. And since it reflects an evaluation of Khrushchev's communicative behavior as unworthy of any statesman, it can only be expected to have reinforced Soviet sensitivity to suggestions of inferiority in comparison with the United States.

5.4. Misunderstanding: Whose responsibility?

Misunderstandings are certainly not only the newspaper's responsibility. The purpose of this paragraph is simply to ask the question in its title. By addressing it to an audience of (among others) linguists, it is hoped that it will stimulate some soul-searching among one group of scholars who would much rather avoid the issue, and another group of those who thought they knew the answer.

FOOTNOTES

1. This does not mean that earlier reporting practices cannot be discussed in terms of 'objectivity'. Cf. D. Schiller's (1981) account of the nineteenth-century American penny press.

2. For further documentation of this episode in the American press coverage of the U.S.S.R., see W.H. Chamberlin (1942, 1944), P. Willen (1954), J.L. Gaddis (1972: 34ff.), and R. Polenberg (1972: 40).

3. M. Schudson (1978: 149) quotes Luce as saying, while advocating a blend of fact and opinion in a news magazine: "Show me a man who thinks he's objective, and I'll show you a man who's deceiving himself."

4. For a proper use of the term in a critical approach to what we do with language, see D. Bolinger (1980: 59-60).

5. The article gives the abbreviation F.L.N.C. Jalbert misquotes (and keeps referring to) it as F.I.N.C. The 'correct' abbreviation is F.N.L.C. (standing for 'Front National de Libération Congolais').

6. The neologism *verbial* was first introduced in Verschueren (1979), on the analogy of the word 'adverbial', which covers both adverbs and adverb-like expressions. The existing term 'verbal' would not have been suitable because its established meaning is a word that combines characteristics of a verb with those of a noun or adjective, as is the case with gerunds, infinitives, and participles.

7. The essential points of this review of properties of LAVs has been drawn from J. Verschueren (n.d.), where they are discussed in greater detail.

8. Reference is made here to pragmatics viewed as a theory of the adaptability of language, which would allow for the description of any pragmatic phenomenon in terms of objects of adaptation (that which language gets adapted to, i.e. circumstances, beliefs, desires, intentions), levels of adaptation (i.e. levels of linguistic structuring at which adaptation processes take place), stages, degrees, and functions of adaptation.

9. For a discussion of the notion 'prototype' in lexical semantics, and its application to the verb *to lie*, see L. Coleman and P. Kay (1981).

10. This motivation is explained in detail in the first chapter of J. Verschueren (1979).

11. For more details on a project aimed at discovering metapragmatic universals which could be used as a point of reference in the further study of intercultural differences in the conceptualization of verbal behavior, see J. Verschueren (1984a).

12. Both of these aspects are part of what M. Reddy (1979) calls the 'conduit metaphor' in terms of which linguistic activity tends to be conceptualized by speakers of English. Cf. also G. Lakoff and M. Johnson (1980).

13. Such a view is explicitly defended by Edmund S. Glenn (1981). For a review of the issues involved, see J. Verschueren (1984b).

REFERENCES

Bohlen, Charles E.
    1973   *Witness to history, 1929-1969*. New York: W.W. Norton & Company.

Bolinger, Dwight
    1973   "Truth is a linguistic question". *Language* 49:3.539-550.

    1980   *Language — The loaded weapon: The use and abuse of language today*. London: Longman.

Chamberlin, William Henry
    1942   "Russia: An American problem". *The Atlantic Monthly* 169.148-156.

    1944   "Information, *please*, about Russia". *Harper's Magazine* 188.405-412.

Coleman, Linda and Paul Kay
    1981   "Prototype semantics: The English word *lie*". *Language* 57:1.26-44.

Davis, Howard and Paul Walton
    1983   "Death of a premier: consensus and closure in international news". In H. Davis and P. Walton (eds.), 8-49.

Davis, Howard and Paul Walton (eds.)
    1983   *Language, image, media*. Oxford: Basil Blackwell.

Gaddis, John Lewis
    1972   *The United States and the origins of the cold war, 1941-1947*. New York/London: Columbia University Press.

Glasgow University Media Group
    1980   *More bad news*. London: Routledge & Kegan Paul.

Glenn, Edmund S.
    1981   *Man and mankind: Conflict and communication between cultures*. Norwood, N.J.: Ablex.

Hohenberg, John
    1978   *A crisis for the American press*. New York: Columbia University Press.

Jalbert, Paul L.
    1983   "Some constructs for analysing news". In H. Davis and P. Walton (eds.), 282-299.

Kennan, George F.
    1972   *Memoirs, 1950-1963*, Vol. II. Boston: Little, Brown and Company.

Khrushchev, Nikita
:   1970   *Khrushchev remembers*. With an introduction, commentary and notes by Edward Crankshaw. New York: Bantam Books.

Kress, Gunther
:   1983   "Linguistic and ideological transformations in news reporting". In H. Davis and P. Walton (eds.), 120-138.

Lakoff, George and Mark Johnson
:   1980   *Metaphors we live by*. Chicago: University of Chicago Press.

Lippmann, Walter and Charles Merz
:   1920   "A test of the news". Supplement to *The New Republic* 23 (August 4, 1920). 1-42.

Ortony, Andrew (ed.)
:   1979   *Metaphor and thought*. Cambridge: Cambridge University Press.

Polenberg, Richard
:   1972   *War and society: The United States 1941-1945*. Philadelphia: J.B. Lippincott Company.

Psathas, George (ed.)
:   1979   *Everyday language: Studies in ethnomethodology*. New York: Irvington Publishers.

Reddy, Michael J.
:   1979   "The conduit metaphor: A case of frame conflict in our language about language." In A. Ortony (ed.), 284-324.

Sacks, Harvey
:   1972   "An initial investigation of the usability of conversational data for doing sociology". In D. Sudnow (ed.), 31-74.

Schenkein, Jim
:   1979   "The radio raiders story". In G. Psathas (ed.), 187-201.

Schiller, Dan
:   1981   *Objectivity and the news: The public and the rise of commercial journalism*. Philadelphia: University of Pennsylvania Press.

Schudson, Michael
:   1978   *Discovering the news: A social history of American newspapers*. New York: Basic Books.

Sudnow, David (ed.)
:   1972   *Studies in social interaction*. New York: The Free Press.

Verschueren, Jef
:   1979   *What people say they do with words*. University of California, Berkeley, Ph.D. dissertation. Revised and expanded version published as *What people say they do with words: Prolegomena to an empirical-conceptual approach to linguistic action*. Norwood, N.J.: Ablex, 1985.

    1984a   *Basic linguistic action verbs: A questionnaire*. Antwerp Papers in Linguistics 37.

1984b   "Linguistics and crosscultural communication". *Language in Society* 13:4.489-509.

n.d.   "Metapragmatics and universals of linguistic action". In J. Verschueren (ed.), n.d.

Verschueren, Jef (ed.)
  n.d.   *Linguistic action: Some empirical-conceptual studies*. Norwood, NJ: Ablex. (forthcoming)

Wicker, Tom
  1975   *On Press*. New York: Berkley Publishing Corporation.

Wilkinson, Paul
  1979   "Terrorism — Weapon of the weak". *Encyclopaedia Britannica*, 1979 Book of the Year, 129-137.

Willen, Paul
  1954   "Who 'collaborated' with Russia?" *Antioch review* 14.259-283.

Wise, David and Thomas B. Ross
  1962   *The U-2 affair*. London: The Cresset Press.

INDEX

Age: 28, 29
American involvement: 17-18
Angola: 15-16, 18, 20-24
apology: 97
Australia: 28-30
Baker, R.: 88
Baldwin, H.W.: 78
Baluba tribe: 16
Bartlett, E.L.: 54
Belair, F.: 81
Belgian Radio and Television: 7
Belgian troops: 12-18
Belgium's Congolese Army: 15
Bemba tribes: 16
Berlin question: 51
Bohlen, C.: 89, 94, 95, 98
Bolinger, D.: 30, 31
Carroll, R.: 12
Carter, J.: 18
Caruthers, O.: 48, 65, 76, 77
CIA: 75, 81
closure: 25
Collier's: 3
common ground: 9, 13
conceptualization: 38-39
Congolese National Liberation
  Front: 17, 19, 23
consensus: 10, 25, 28
cross-cultural communication:
  38, 42
Cuban advisers: 18, 23-24

Davis, H.: 10, 25-28
Doty, R.C.: 89
Eisenhower, D.D.: 5-6, 33, 41-98
emotionality: 50-51, 54, 63-64,
  82, 90, 91, 93, 96, 98
English: 42, 43
ethnography of communication:
  38
ethnomethodology: 31
euphemism: 31
exclusion: 25-27
eye-witness account: 12-13
face: 90, 97
Frankel, M.: 61, 76, 77, 78, 89, 91
free press: 1-8
French Foreign Legion: 12-18
Gaulle, C. de: 84, 90
Geneva conventions: 23
Germany: 10, 25-26
Glasgow University Media Group:
  9, 26
Goldsborough, J.O.: 12
Goldwater, B.: 3, 5
Great Britain: 10, 25-26
Gromyko, A.: 63
Hadden, B.: 5
Hagerty, J.: 89
Hohenberg, J.: 94
ideology: 4, 7-8, 9-30
implicit meaning: 31
interpretation: 94, 96-97

Jalbert, P.L.:   11-25, 27, 30-31
Johnson, L.B.:   3
Jorden, W.J.:   51, 57, 76, 77, 88
juxtaposition: 20-21
Katanga: 16-17
Katangans: 11-24
Kennan, G.F.:   96
Khrushchev, N.:   33, 41-98
Kinshasa: 16
Kolchak: 5
Kolwezi: 12-16, 19, 21
Kress, G.:   10, 28-30
language: 9-32
Life: 3
linguistic action verbial: 34
Lippmann, W.:   2, 4, 8
Lockheed: 45, 54
Luba tribes: 16
Luce, H.:   5
Lunda tribes: 16, 20, 24
lying: 35, 37
Macmillan, H.:   41, 84, 90, 97, 98
manipulation: 10, 31, 93
Marxism: 20-24
membership categorization: 11, 14-24
Merz, C.:   4, 8
metaphor: 14, 43
metapragmatic description: 39, 43, 45-94, 98
metapragmatic metaphor: 38-39, 47-94
metapragmatic term: 34-39
Middleton, D.:   83
mining interests: 16-17, 18
Mobutu Sese Seko: 12-24
Moro, A.:   10, 25-27
mutual knowledge: 8

NASA: 45, 47, 53, 55, 56, 58, 93
News: 28-29
news consumption: 6-7
news event: 1-2
news reporting: 3-6, 94-99
news value: 94
Newsweek: 11-24
New York Times: 2, 3, 4, 33, 41-99
Nixon, R.:   48
nominalization: 28-30
objectivity: 1-8, 95
Paris summit: 33, 41, 48, 51, 64, 70, 75, 78, 82-91, 93, 96
peaceful coexistence: 41
political-communicative event: 41, 93
political maneuvering: 64, 72, 79-80, 93
Powers, F.G.:   45, 53, 58
Pringle, J.:   12-13
pseudo-event: 7
public interest: 3, 94
public opinion: 6
quotation: 43, 50
Raymond, J.:   45, 58, 73, 76, 77
Reagan administration: 22
Red Brigades: 25-27, 31
reification: 17
reported speech: 43, 50, 68
Reston, J.:   69, 76, 77, 78, 80, 86, 93, 94, 95, 96
Rosenthal, A.M.:   88
Ross, T.B.:   94
Russian: 42, 43
Russian Revolution: 4-5, 95
Sacks, H.:   11
Salisbury, H.:   3, 8, 89, 96

INDEX

Schenkein, J.: 31
Schiller, D.: 8
Schmidt, D. Adams: 78
Schudson, M.: 1, 3, 94
Security Council: 55
semi-quote: 43, 47, 50, 54, 58, 63, 64, 68, 72, 74-75
Shaba: 11-24
Soviet involvement: 17-18
Soviet Union: 3, 22, 33, 41-98
Stevenson, A.: 88, 90, 91
style of communication: 68-69, 80, 90, 93, 98
Swahili: 17
television news: 10, 25-28
terrorism: 27-28
Thompson, L.E.: 53
Time (magazine): 5, 11, 19-24

truth: 47, 64, 68, 81, 94-96
Tshombé, M.: 16, 24
Turkey: 45, 56, 93
U-2 incident: 33, 39, 41-99
understanding: 94, 97-99
United Nations: 16, 95
United States: 10, 25, 33, 41-98
verb of perception: 47
verifiability: 1-2, 7
Vietnam: 3, 30
Walton, P.: 10, 25-28
Webster's: 1, 2
Wicker, T.: 3, 5-6, 7
Wise, D.: 94
World War II: 3, 6
Zaïre: 11-24, 31
Zambia: 20

In the PRAGMATICS & BEYOND series the following monographs have been published thus far:

I:1. *Anca M. Nemoianu*: The Boat's Gonna Leave: A Study of Children Learning a Second Language from Conversations with Other Children.
Amsterdam, 1980, vi, 116 pp. Paperbound.

I:2. *Michael D. Fortescue*: A Discourse Production Model for 'Twenty Questions'.
Amsterdam, 1980, x, 137 pp. Paperbound.

I:3. *Melvin Joseph Adler*: A Pragmatic Logic for Commands.
Amsterdam, 1980, viii, 131 pp. Paperbound.

I:4. *Jef Verschueren*: On Speech Act Verbs.
Amsterdam, 1980, viii, 83 pp. Paperbound.

I:5. *Geoffrey N. Leech*: Explorations in Semantics and Pragmatics.
Amsterdam, 1980, viii, 133 pp. Paperbound. Temporarily out of print.

I:6. *Herman Parret*: Contexts of Understanding.
Amsterdam, 1980, viii, 109 pp. Paperbound.

I:7. *Benoît de Cornulier*: Meaning Detachment.
Amsterdam, 1980, vi, 124 pp. Paperbound.

I:8. *Peter Eglin*: Talk and Taxonomy: A methodological comparison of ethnosemantics and ethnomethodology with reference to terms for Canadian doctors.
Amsterdam, 1980, x, 125 pp. Paperbound.

II:1. *John Dinsmore*: The Inheritance of Presupposition.
Amsterdam, 1981, vi, 97 pp. Paperbound.

II:2. *Charles Travis*: The True and the False: The Domain of the Pragmatic.
Amsterdam, 1981, vi, 164 pp. Paperbound.

II:3. *Johan Van der Auwera*: What do we talk about when we talk? Speculative grammar and the semantics and pragmatics of focus.
Amsterdam, 1981, vi, 121 pp. Paperbound.

II:4. *Joseph F. Kess & Ronald A. Hoppe*: Ambiguity in Psycholinguistics.
Amsterdam, 1981, v, 123 pp. Paperbound.

II:5. *Karl Sornig*: Lexical Innovation: A Study of Slang, Colloquialisms and Casual Speech.
Amsterdam, 1981, viii, 117 pp. Paperbound.

II:6. *Knud Lambrecht*: Topic, Antitopic and Verb Agreement in Non-Standard French.
Amsterdam, 1981, vii, 113 pp. Paperbound.

II:7. *Jan-Ola Östman*: You Know: A Discourse-Functional Study.
Amsterdam, 1981, viii, 91 pp. Paperbound.

II:8. *Claude Zilberberg*: Essai sur les modalités tensives.
Amsterdam, 1981, xi, 154 pp. + 4 folding tables. Paperbound.

III:1. *Ivan Fonagy*: Situation et Signification.
Amsterdam, 1982, v, 160 pp. Paperbound.

III:2/3. *Jürgen Weissenborn and Wolfgang Klein (eds.)*: Here and There. Cross-linguistic Studies in Deixis and Demonstration.
Amsterdam, 1982. v, 296 pp. Paperbound.

III:4. *Waltraud Brennenstuhl*: Control and Ability. Towards a Biocybernetics of Language.
Amsterdam, 1982. v, 123 pp. Paperbound.

III:5. *Wolfgang Wildgen*: Catastrophe Theoretic Semantics: An Elaboration and Application of René Thom's Theory.
Amsterdam, 1982. iv, 124 pp. Paperbound.

III:6. *René Dirven, Louis Goossens, Yvan Putseys and Emma Vorlat*: The Scene of Linguistic Action and its Perspectivization by SPEAK, TALK, SAY and TELL.
Amsterdam, 1982. v, 186 pp. Paperbound.

III:7. *Thomas Ballmer*: Biological Foundations of Linguistic Communication. Towards a Biocybernetics of Language.
Amsterdam, 1982. x, 161 pp. Paperbound.

III:8. *Douglas N. Walton*: Topical Relevance in Argumentation.
Amsterdam, 1982. viii, 81 pp. Paperbound.

IV:1. *Marcelo Dascal*: Pragmatics and the Philosophy of Mind. Vol. I.
Amsterdam, 1983. xii, 207 pp. Paperbound.

IV:2. *Richard Zuber*: Non-declarative Sentences.
Amsterdam, 1983. ix, 123 pp. Paperbound.

IV:3. *Michel Meyer*: Meaning and Reading. A Philosophical Essay on Language and Literature.
Amsterdam, 1983. ix, 176 pp. Paperbound.

IV:4. *Walburga von Raffler-Engel*: The Perception of Nonverbal Behavior in the Career Interview.
Amsterdam, 1983. viii, 148 pp. Paperbound.

IV:5. *Jan Prucha*: Pragmalinguistics: East European Approaches.
Amsterdam, 1983. v, 103 pp. Paperbound.

IV:6. *Alex Huebler*: Understatements and Hedges in English.
Amsterdam, 1983. ix, 192 pp. Paperbound.

IV:7. *Herman Parret*: Semiotics and Pragmatics. An Evaluative Comparison of Conceptual Frameworks.
Amsterdam, 1983. xii, 136 pp. Paperbound.

IV:8. *Jürgen Streeck*: Social Order in Child Communication. A Study in Microethnography.
Amsterdam, 1983. vii, 130 pp. Paperbound.

V:1. *Marlene Dolitsky*: Under the Tumtum Tree: From Nonsense to Sense, a Study in Non-automatic Comprehension.
Amsterdam, 1984. vii, 119 pp. Paperbound.

V:2. *Roger G. van de Velde*: Prolegomena to Inferential Discourse Processing.
Amsterdam, 1984. viii, 100 pp. Paperbound.

V:3. *Teun Van Dijk*: Prejudice in Discourse. An Analysis of Ethnic Prejudice in Cognition and Conversation.
Amsterdam, 1984. x, 170 pp. Paperbound.

V:4. *Henk Haverkate*: Speech Acts, Speakers and Hearers. Reference and Referential Strategies in Spanish.
Amsterdam, 1984. xi, 142 pp. Paperbound.

V:5. *Lauri Carlson*: "Well" in Dialogue Games: A Discourse Analysis of the Interjection "Well" in Idealized Conversation.
Amsterdam, 1984 (publ. 1985). ix, 111 pp. Paperbd.

V:6. *Danilo Marcondes de Souza Filho*: Language and Action: A Reassessment of Speech Act Theory.
Amsterdam, 1984 (publ. 1985). ix, 167 pp. Paperbd.

V:7. *Lars Qvortrup*: The Social Significance of Telematics: An Essay on the Information Society.
Amsterdam, 1984 (publ. 1985). xi, 230 pp. Paperbd.
V:8. *J.C.P. Auer*: Bilingual Conversation.
Amsterdam, 1984 (publ. 1985). ix, 116 pp. Paperbd.
VI:1. *Jean-Pierre Desclés, Zlatka Guentchéva & Sebastian Shaumyan*: Theoretical Aspects of Passivization in the Framework of Applicative Grammar.
Amsterdam, 1985 (publ. 1986). viii, 115 pp. Paperbd.
VI:2. *Jon-K Adams*: Pragmatics and Fiction.
Amsterdam, 1985 (publ. 1986). vi, 77 pp. Paperbd.
VI:3. *Betsy K. Barnes*: The Pragmatics of Left Detachment in Spoken Standard French.
Amsterdam, 1985 (publ. 1986). viii, 123 pp. Paperbd.
VI:4. *Luigia Camaioni, Cláudia de Lemos, et al.*: Questions on Social Explanation: Piagetian Themes reconsidered.
Amsterdam, 1985 (publ. 1986). viii, 141 pp. Paperbd.
VI:5. *Jef Verschueren*: International News Reporting: Metapragmatic Metaphors and the U-2.
Amsterdam, 1985 (publ. 1986). viii, 105 pp. Paperbd.
VI:6. *Sharon Sabsay, Martha Platt, et al.*: Social Setting, Stigma, and Communicative Competence: Explorations of the Conversational Interactions of Retarded Adults.
Amsterdam, 1985 (publ. 1986). v, 137 pp. Paperbd.
VI:7. *Nira Reiss*: Speech Act Taxonomy as a Tool for Ethnographic Description: An Analysis Based on Videotapes of Continuous Behavior in two New York Household.
Amsterdam, 1985 (publ. 1986). ix, 153 pp. Paperbd.
VI:8. *Saleh M. Suleiman*: Jordanian Arabic Between Diglossia and Bilingualism: Linguistic Analysis.
Amsterdam, 1985 (publ. 1986). xvi, 131 pp. Paperbd.